CYPRUS, GREECE, AND MALTA

CYPRUS, GREECE, AND MALTA

EDITED BY NOAH TESCH, ASSISTANT EDITOR, GEOGRAPHY

Britannica®
Educational Publishing

IN ASSOCIATION WITH

ROSEN
EDUCATIONAL SERVICES

Published in 2014 by Britannica Educational Publishing
(a trademark of Encyclopædia Britannica, Inc.)
in association with Rosen Educational Services, LLC
29 East 21st Street, New York, NY 10010.

For a listing of additional Britannica Educational Publishing titles, call toll free (800) 237-9932.

First Edition

Britannica Educational Publishing
J.E. Luebering: Director, Core Reference Group
Adam Augustyn: Assistant Manager, Core Reference Group
Marilyn L. Barton: Senior Coordinator, Production Control
Steven Bosco: Director, Editorial Technologies
Lisa S. Braucher: Senior Producer and Data Editor
Yvette Charboneau: Senior Copy Editor
Kathy Nakamura: Manager, Media Acquisition
Edited by: Noah Tesch, Assistant Editor, Geography

Rosen Educational Services
Jeanne Nagle: Senior Editor
Nelson Sá: Art Director
Cindy Reiman: Photo Researcher
Brian Garvey: Designer, Cover Design
Introduction by Richard Barrington

Library of Congress Cataloging-in-Publication Data

Tesch, Noah.
Cyprus, Greece, and Malta/edited by Noah Tesch. — 1st ed.
        p. cm. — (The Britannica guide to countries of the European Union)
"In association with Britannica Educational Publishing, Rosen Educational Services."
Includes bibliographic references and index.
ISBN 978-1-61530-972-6 (library binding)
1. European Union—Cyprus—Juvenile literature. 2. European Union—Greece—Juvenile
literature. 3. European Union—Malta—Juvenile literature. 4. Cyprus--Juvenile literature. 5.
Greece—Juvenile literature. 6. Malta—Juvenile literature. I. Tesch, Noah. II. Title.
DS54.A3 C977 2014
956.93—dc23

Manufactured in the United States of America

On the cover: View of the Greek Parliament on Syntagma Square, in Athens. © *iStockphoto.
com/Arpad Benedek*

Cover, p. iii (map contour and stars), back cover, multiple interior pages (stars) ©iStock-
photo.com/pop_jop; cover, multiple interior pages (background graphic) Mina De La O/
Digital Vision/Getty Images

CONTENTS

8/17

21

29

33

CHAPTER 12: GREECE SINCE WORLD WAR I **123**

112

115

124

Map of the Mediterranean, featuring Cyprus, Greece, and Malta. Olinchuk/Shutterstock.com.

Since ancient times, Greece has been central to the story of mankind. European civilization has been shaped almost immeasurably by the philosophical, political, and artistic works of the societies that flourished in the area of the Aegean Sea beginning in the 2nd millennium BCE. This cultural legacy survived and evolved in Greece beyond the end of the classical period, even though Greece was then absorbed into a series of larger empires before emerging as a modern state in the early 19th century. This book introduces readers not only to Greece but also to Cyprus and Malta, island countries that were also among the earliest sites of civilization in Europe. They also share with Greece a rugged landscape, Mediterranean climate, and membership in the European Union (EU).

Although Cyprus is considered part of Europe, its location at the extreme eastern side of the Mediterranean places it much closer to the Middle Eastern countries of Syria and Lebanon, and the Asian portion of Turkey, than to any European country. Although the island is relatively small—its length is just 140 miles (225 km)—Cyprus features quite a varied landscape, with mountain ranges to the north and south framing a low-lying plain in the centre. Cyprus also has beautiful sandy beaches around its coastline, which help make it a popular European vacation destination.

The population of Cyprus is made up of an ethnic Greek majority and an ethnic Turkish minority. Today, the island is partitioned between the two groups, with the Turkish minority in the northern portion of the island having declared its sector an independent country. Turkey is the only country to have recognized this declaration. The Turkish and Greek portions of Cyprus cooperate on some practical matters, but overall the division has hampered the economic development of the island.

The first settlements on Cyprus date back some 9,000 years. Greek influence had begun by the first millennium BCE, and Greek language and culture quickly became a dominant presence on the island. In subsequent centuries, Cyprus was caught up in the region's changing political and military fortunes, passing through periods of Assyrian, Egyptian, Persian, and Roman rule. This pattern persisted throughout most of the island's history, although an independent monarchy reigned in the 13th and 14th centuries.

In the early 20th century, a long period of domination by the Ottoman Empire gave way to British rule. Following World War II, Britain pursued a policy of decolonization, which led to two distinct possible paths for the future of Cyprus: independence or union with Greece. Many in the ethnic Greek community favoured becoming part of Greece, but the Turkish Cypriots were violently opposed. The two sides

eventually agreed on a compromise that led to the creation of an independent Cypriot Republic in 1960. However, they struggled to share power once the plan was implemented. Continuing tensions between Greek and Turkish factions led Turkey to invade Cyprus in 1974; Turkish troops succeeded in capturing the northern third of the country before a cease-fire was declared. Despite repeated objections by the United Nations, this Turkish sector of the island has effectively operated as a separate state ever since. The Greek portion of the island was granted admission to the EU in 2004. Other EU member countries have advocated for the reunification of Cyprus. Although the EU won a Nobel Peace Prize in 2012 for its efforts to create harmony among European countries, it remains to be seen whether its diplomatic abilities will succeed in mending the rift between the Greek and Turkish sectors.

In the 21st century, Greece has featured prominently in world affairs owing to its central role in the European debt crisis. Following the financial and economic crises of 2008-09, it became clear that Greece was in danger of defaulting on its debts. Other European countries became involved in trying to help Greece work through its debt problem because Greece is a member of the euro currency zone and financial institutions in several major countries are holders of Greek debt. The process has at times pitted creditors demanding payment against the Greek people, who resisted the tax increases and cuts in public spending required under the terms of the rescue package. These problems have shattered the Greek economy and threaten to damage the international value of the euro for years to come.

For much of its history since the classical period, Greece has been ruled by outside powers. Greece came under Roman control in the 2nd century BCE, and later became part of the Byzantine Empire, Rome's successor in Eastern Europe and the Middle East. Greece is a mountainous nation with more than 2,000 islands, which not only makes travel and communication within the country difficult, but has necessitated that it be governed as separate provinces rather than a unified whole. In the 5th and 6th centuries, Greece suffered a series of raids by foreign invaders, as well as other hardships such as plague. The economic and political disruption caused by these events made it more difficult for the Byzantine Empire to keep control of the small and widely scattered communities of the Greek interior. Instead imperial administration focused on large, well-fortified cities and coastal regions. The Byzantine Empire reconquered many areas of Greece in the 9th and 10th centuries.

The divisions within Greece became deeper when the Fourth Crusade, launched by the Western Christian church at the end of the 12th century, turned its attention away from Jerusalem and attacked the Byzantine Empire instead. After the crusaders captured Constantinople in 1204, many regions of Greece came under Frankish and Venetian rule, while other regions remained under Byzantine control.

By the middle of the 13th century, the Byzantine Empire had lost nearly all of its territory outside of the Greek-speaking lands of the Aegean region. This loss of ethnic diversity, coupled with the threats posed by Turkish and Western invaders, helped strengthen the sense of Greek identity within the remaining Byzantine territories. Meanwhile, Greek-speaking scholars developed a new interest in ancient Greek texts and extolled the glories of ancient Greek civilization in their writings.

The Ottoman Empire conquered much of Eastern Europe, including Greece, in the 15th century and would continue to dominate the area until the 19th century. It was under Ottoman rule that the idea of Greek ethnic identity spread and eventually evolved into a nationalist independence movement. The Ottoman system of government had organized the empire along religious lines and relied heavily on non-Muslim religious leaders to administer their territories.

By the 18th century, the Ottoman Empire was in decline, while various classes of Greek society were gaining political, economic, and intellectual power. Slowly, the notion of Greek independence began to gather momentum, with armed rebellions occurring sporadically throughout the early 19th century. A full-fledged revolt broke out in 1821. There were violent skirmishes between different factions of the Greek rebels even before they had fully driven away the Ottomans, but with the assistance of Britain, France, and Russia, an independent Greek state was established in 1827.

The first century or so of Greek independence was marked by internal conflicts and outside interference by the major powers of Europe. Despite the apparent fragility of the new state, Greece embarked on a program known as the "Great Idea," which sought to expand the borders of the Greek state to include all the areas of the Ottoman Empire where Greeks lived. This led to a series of economically disastrous conflicts. As a result, an international commission was appointed in 1897 to oversee the repayment of Greece's foreign debts—a situation similar to Greece's 21st- century financial woes within the EU.

Political upheaval was a regular part of Greek life in the 20th century. Internal political divisions were intense, and over time the country lurched between monarchy and democracy, and between right-wing dictatorship and communism. Today, the country is once again a democracy, but fiscal mismanagement by the government has contributed heavily to Greece's recent debt crisis. In the future, it seems that solving the financial crisis will require Greece to remedy two recurring problems—internal divisions and conflicts with other countries.

Although Malta is much smaller than Greece or Cyprus, its location in the centre of the Mediterranean has given it an important role in history. Over the centuries, Malta has been occupied and ruled by a series of powerful foreign states as they sought to extend their influence. For this reason, Maltese culture is a product of European, North African, and Middle Eastern influences.

Malta is an archipelago, or a group of islands, which lies just south of the western end of Sicily. Because the country consists of five small islands, Malta has an extensive coastline relative to its land area. Much of this coastline is forbidding, consisting of steep limestone formations. Malta's small size and rocky terrain have limited the country's agricultural options, making it heavily reliant on imports. Attempts to modernize and diversify the economy in recent years have included the introduction of light manufacturing, especially within the pharmaceutical industry.

Historically, the key to Malta's prominence has not been its economy but its strategic location. Maltese history has been shaped by the many Mediterranean powers that have reached its shores. There is evidence of Phoenician settlement on Malta between the 8th and 6th centuries BCE, and in the 6th century BCE the island came under the control of Carthage, itself a former Phoenician colony. Rome took possession of Malta during the Second Punic War (218–201 BCE). It is believed that Christianity was introduced to Malta during the Roman era, after the apostle Paul was rescued from a shipwreck in 60 CE.

Over the centuries, the island passed through the hands of a variety of rulers. The Byzantine Empire succeeded the Romans, after which there were periods when Malta was under Arab, Norman, and Spanish rule. Then, in the 16th century, the Holy Roman Emperor Charles V gave Malta to the Knights of Rhodes (later the Knights of Malta), a religious and military order of the Catholic Church. The Knights of Rhodes acquired great riches, mostly via skirmishes with ships of the Ottoman Empire, but largely kept themselves apart from the native Maltese people. The Knights' rule ended when the island was captured by Napoleon Bonaparte at the end of the 18th century. The French were soon expelled by the British, and the area remained a British colony through the 19th and most of the 20th century.

Malta's location made it a valuable asset for the British military. It was an important base for the British fleet during the Crimean War and World War I, and it withstood heavy bombardment by the Axis Powers during World War II. It remained a British military base until 1979. By then, Malta had been granted its independence (in 1964). The country's political and economic development was marked by its admission to the EU in 2004 and the euro currency zone in 2008.

Despite their individual traditions and cultures, Cyprus, Greece, and Malta all show the extent to which the Mediterranean has been a busy crossroads of history. This book provides the details that reveal how history has shaped these countries and how they in turn have influenced history.

CHAPTER 1

CYPRUS: THE LAND AND ITS PEOPLE

C yprus is an island in the eastern Mediterranean Sea that has been renowned since ancient times for its mineral wealth, superb wines and produce, and natural beauty.

A "golden-green leaf thrown into the Sea" and a land of "wild weather and volcanoes," in the words of the Greek Cypriot poet Leonidas Malenis, Cyprus comprises tall mountains, fertile valleys, and wide beaches. Settled for more than 10 millennia, Cyprus stands at a cultural, linguistic, and historic crossroads between Europe and Asia. Its chief cities—the capital of Nicosia, Limassol, Famagusta, and Paphos—have absorbed the influences of generations of conquerors, pilgrims, and travelers and have an air that is both cosmopolitan and provincial. Today Cyprus is a popular tourist destination for visitors from Europe, favoured by honeymooners (as befits the legendary home of Aphrodite, the ancient Greek goddess of love), bird-watchers drawn by the island's diversity of migratory species, and other vacationers.

In 1960 Cyprus became independent of Britain (it had been a crown colony since 1925) as the Republic of Cyprus. The long-standing conflict between the Greek Cypriot majority and the Turkish Cypriot minority and an invasion of the island by Turkish troops in 1974 produced an actual—although internationally unrecognized—partition

The flag of Cyprus. Encyclopaedia Britannica, Inc.

Petra tou Romiou, the legendary site of Aphrodite's emergence from the sea, near Old Paphos, Cyprus. © Berlitz—CLICK/Chicago

of mainland Greece. Its maximum length, from Cape Arnauti in the west to Cape Apostolos Andreas at the end of the northeastern peninsula, is 140 miles (225 km); the maximum north-south extent is 60 miles (100 km). It is the third largest Mediterranean island, after Sicily and Sardinia.

RELIEF

The rugged island of Cyprus resembles a saucepan, with the handle extending northeastward from the main part. The general pattern of its roughly 400-mile (640-km) coastline is indented and rocky, with long, sandy beaches. The Kyrenia Mountains—the western portion of which is also known as the Pentadaktylos for its five-fingered peak—extend for 100 miles (160 km) parallel to and just inland from the northern coast. It is the southernmost range of the great Alpine-Himalayan chain in the eastern Mediterranean; like much of that extensive mountain belt, it is formed largely of deformed masses of Mesozoic limestone.

The Troodos Mountains in the south and southwest are of great interest to geologists, who have concluded that the range, made up of igneous rock, was formed from molten rock beneath the deep ocean (Tethys) that once separated the continents of Eurasia and Afro-Arabia. The range stretches eastward about 50 miles (80 km) from near the island's west coast to the 2,260-foot (689-metre) Stavrovouni peak, about 12 miles (19 km) from the southeastern coast. The range's summit, Mount Olympus (also

of the island and led to the establishment in 1975 of a de facto Turkish Cypriot state in the northern third of the country. The Turkish Cypriot state made a unilateral declaration of independence in 1983 and adopted the name Turkish Republic of Northern Cyprus. Its independence was recognized only by Turkey.

Cyprus lies about 40 miles (65 km) south of Turkey, 60 miles (100 km) west of Syria, and 480 miles (770 km) southeast

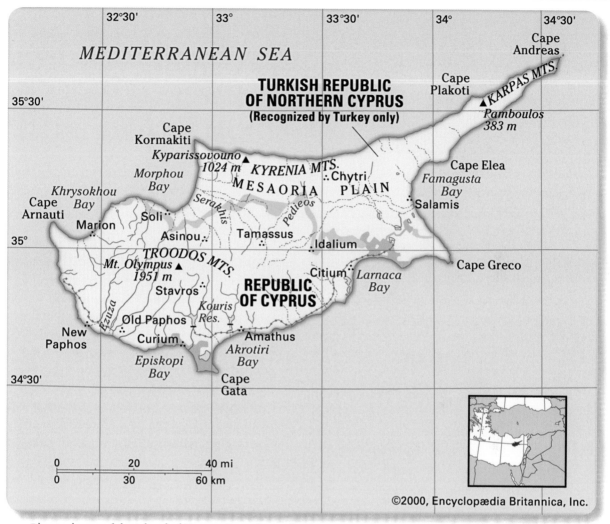

Physical map of the island of Cyprus. Encyclopaedia Britannica, Inc.

called Mount Troodos), reaches an elevation of 6,401 feet (1,951 metres) and is the island's highest point.

Between the two ranges lies the Mesaoria Plain (its name means "Between the Mountains"), which is flat and low-lying and extends from Morphou Bay in the west to Famagusta Bay in the east. Roughly in the centre of the plain is Nicosia. The plain is the principal cereal-growing area in the island.

DRAINAGE AND SOILS

The major rivers in Cyprus originate in the Troodos Mountains. The Pedieos, which is the largest, flows eastward toward Famagusta Bay; the Serakhis flows northwestward and the Karyotis northward to Morphou Bay; and the Kouris flows southward to Episkopi Bay. The rivers are fed entirely from the runoff of winter precipitation; in summer they become dry courses. The island's major soil types consist of imperfect, gravelly lithosols found in the Troodos and Kyrenia mountains and agriculturally productive vertisols located in the Mesaoria Plain and along the southeastern coast. Other, less-productive soils include solonchaks and solonetz soils. These latter are found only in isolated saline pockets throughout the island.

CLIMATE

Cyprus has an intense Mediterranean climate, with a typically strongly marked seasonal rhythm. Hot, dry summers (June to September) and rainy winters (November to March) are separated by short autumn and spring seasons (October and April to May, respectively) of rapid change. Autumn and winter precipitation, on which agriculture and water supply depend, is variable. Average annual precipitation is about 20 inches (500 mm). The lowest average precipitation of 14 inches (350 mm) occurs at Nicosia, and the highest, 41 inches (1,050 mm), is on Mount Olympus. Summer temperatures in Nicosia range between an average daily maximum of 98 °F (37 °C) and an average daily minimum of 70 °F (21 °C); in winter the range is between

59 °F (15 °C) and 41 °F (5 °C). From December to March the Troodos range experiences several weeks of below-freezing night temperatures, and snowfall is considerable.

PLANT AND ANIMAL LIFE

Fossil remains of elephants and hippopotamuses have been found in the Kyrenia area, and in ancient times there were large numbers of deer and boar. The only large wild animal now surviving is the agrino, a subspecies of wild sheep related to the mouflon of the western Mediterranean; it is under strict protection in a small forested area of the Troodos range. Small game is abundant but keenly hunted. Snakes were widespread in ancient times, giving the island the name Ophiussa, "the Abode of Snakes"; they are now relatively rare. Green and loggerhead turtles, which are protected by law, breed on the beaches along the coast.

There is a narrow fertile plain along the northern coast, where the vegetation is largely evergreen and includes olive, carob, and citrus trees. The Troodos range has pine, dwarf oak, cypress, and cedar forest coverings. The southern and western slopes are extensively planted with vineyards. Between autumn and spring the Mesaoria Plain is green and colourful, with an abundance of wildflowers, flowering bushes, and shrubs; there are also patches of woodland in which eucalyptus and various types of acacia, cypress, and lowland pine are found. Orange plantations dot the island's northwestern end in the area around Morphou.

Cyprus lies on major migration routes for birds. In spring and autumn millions pass over the island, while many species winter there. Among the numerous resident species are francolin and chukar partridges.

ETHNIC GROUPS AND LANGUAGES

The people of Cyprus represent two main ethnic groups, Greek and Turkish. The Greek Cypriots, who constitute nearly four-fifths of the population, descended from a mixture of aboriginal inhabitants and immigrants from the Peloponnese who colonized Cyprus starting about 1200 BCE and assimilated subsequent settlers up to the 16th century. Roughly one-fifth of the population are Turkish Cypriots, descendants of the soldiers of the Ottoman army that conquered the island in 1571 and of immigrants from Anatolia brought in by the sultan's government. Since 1974 additional immigrants from Turkey have been brought in to work vacant land and increase the total labour force.

The language of the majority is Greek and of the minority, Turkish. There are also a small number of Arabic-speaking Maronite Christians, as well as a small group who speak Armenian. These groups each total only a few thousand speakers, and they are mostly bilingual, with either Turkish or Greek their second language. English is widely spoken and understood. Illiteracy is extremely low, the result of an excellent educational system.

RELIGION

The Greek Cypriots are primarily Eastern Orthodox Christians. Their church, the Church of Cyprus, is autocephalous (not under the authority of any patriarch); this privilege was granted to Archbishop Anthemius in BCE 488 by the Byzantine emperor Zeno. Under the Ottoman Empire, the archbishop of the Church of Cyprus was made responsible for the secular as well as the religious behaviour of the Orthodox community and given the

CHURCH OF CYPRUS

The Church of Cyprus, also called the Orthodox Church of Cyprus, is one of the oldest autocephalous, or ecclesiastically independent, churches of the Eastern Orthodox communion. Its independence, first recognized by the third ecumenical Council of Ephesus (431), was reaffirmed by the Council in Trullo (692) and was never lost, not even during the occupation of the island by the crusaders. Under the feudal French dynasty of the Lusignans (1191–1489) and the Venetians (1489–1571), the efforts of the Latin bishops to submit the Orthodox Church of Cyprus to the pope's authority were unsuccessful. Until the Turkish conquest of the island in

1571, the Greek bishops were often submitted to the authority of the Latin archbishop and forced to serve as auxiliaries of their Latin colleagues.

The highest ecclesiastical authority lay with the synod, composed of the archbishop of Nicosia and the three other bishops of the island—Paphos, Citium, and Kyrenia—who were, and still are, elected by both clergy and laity, each of the four bishoprics being divided into several parishes.

The bishops became the natural leaders of national resistance: during the Greek War of Independence (1821–32), all the bishops on the island, as well as several abbots, were hanged by the Turks, while in the years of British control (1878–1958), the bishops took an active lead in the Greek Cypriot movement for union with Greece (*énosis*). In 1956 the Archbishop Makarios and the Bishop of Kyrenia were exiled by the British. When the new Cypriot republic became independent in 1960, the church was assured of its position as an autocephalous and independent Greek Orthodox Church on the basis of its old titles, and Archbishop Makarios was elected the first president of the new republic.

Monastic life has developed greatly since the beginning of the republic. There are several monasteries, the most important being the monastery of Kykkou. Parish clergy are educated in an undergraduate seminary; higher theological education is obtained at the University of Athens. The church keeps several educational and philanthropic institutions and publishes *Apostolos Barnabas,* a monthly ecclesiastical–theological review.

title ethnarch. The Turkish Cypriots are Sunni Muslims. There are also smaller Maronite, Armenian, Roman Catholic, and Anglican Christian communities on the island.

SETTLEMENT PATTERNS

The Cypriots were traditionally a largely rural people, but a steady drift toward towns began in the early 20th century. The census of 1973 recorded six towns, defined as settlements of more than 5,000 inhabitants, and nearly 600 villages. Following the Turkish occupation in 1974 of the northern portion of the island, this pattern changed, the result of the need to resettle some 180,000 Greek Cypriot refugees who had fled from the Turkish-controlled area to the southern part of the island. The accommodations built for them were situated mainly in the neighbourhood of the three towns south of the line of demarcation, particularly in the Nicosia suburban area, which was still controlled by the government of the Republic of Cyprus. In contrast, the northern portion of the island is now more sparsely populated despite the influx of Turkish Cypriots from the south and the introduction of Turkish settlers from the mainland.

The six towns recorded in the 1973 census, under the undivided republic, were the headquarters of the island's six administrative districts. Of these Kyrenia (Turkish: Girne), Famagusta (Greek:

NICOSIA

Nicosia (Turkish: LefkosŞa), the capital of the Republic of Cyprus, lies along the Pedieos River, in the centre of the Mesaoria Plain between the Kyrenia Mountains (north) and the Troodos range (south). The city is also the archiepiscopal seat of the autocephalous (having the right to elect its own archbishop and bishops) Church of Cyprus.

Nicosia came successively under the control of the Byzantines (330–1191), the Lusignan kings (1192–1489), the Venetians (1489–1571), the Turks (1571–1878), and the British (1878–1960), and thus reflects the vicissitudes of Cypriot history and both Eastern and Western influences. Nicosia, known in antiquity as Ledra, is a medieval corruption of the Byzantine name Lefkosia. The city was a kingdom in the 7th century BCE and has been a bishopric from the 4th century CE. It has been the seat of government of Cyprus since the 10th century. The city's walled fortifications, originally erected by the Lusignan kings and later rebuilt by the Venetians to encompass a smaller area (3 miles [5 km] round), did not prevent invasions by the Genoese in

The town hall in Nicosia, Cyprus. © Georgios Alexandris/Fotolia

1373, the Mamlūks in 1426, and the Turks in 1570. Standing in mute testimony to the religious and political changes of the city is the Cathedral of St. Sophia. Begun in 1209, completed in 1325, and pillaged by invaders, it was converted into the chief mosque of Cyprus in 1571. In 1954 its name was changed to the Selimiye Mosque in honour of the Ottoman sultan Selim II, under whose reign Cyprus was conquered.

During the 20th century the city boundaries were extended beyond the existing circular Venetian walls, and the old town within them was rebuilt. As a result of the Turkish intervention in 1974, part of the northern section of Nicosia, including the former international airport, has remained within the United Nations Forces in Cyprus operational boundary separating the Republic of Cyprus (south) from the Turkish Cypriot-administered areas (north). The city experienced an influx of an estimated 35,000 Greek Cypriot refugees from the north in the mid-1970s.

Nicosia's light industries, mainly serving the local market, include the manufacture and processing of cotton yarns and textiles, cigarettes, flour, confectionery, soft drinks, footwear, and clothing. Nicosia is connected by good roads with the other major towns of the island. A new international airport was established in 1974 at Larnaca, about 21 miles (34 km) southeast of Nicosia. The Cyprus Museum in the city houses many archaeological treasures. Most of the population in the surrounding area is engaged in agriculture, and crops produced include wheat, barley, vegetables, and fruits; goats and sheep are also raised.

Ammókhostos; Turkish: Mağusa), and the northern half of Nicosia are to the north of the demarcation line drawn in 1974 and are in Turkish Cypriot hands; that part of Nicosia is the administrative centre of the Turkish Cypriot sector. Limassol, Larnaca, Paphos, and the southern part of Nicosia remained in Greek Cypriot hands after 1974; that part of Nicosia is the nominal capital of the entire Republic of Cyprus and the administrative centre of the Greek Cypriot sector.

DEMOGRAPHIC TRENDS

At times Cypriots have emigrated in large numbers, and it is estimated that as many live abroad as on the island itself. The great majority of emigrants have gone to the United Kingdom or to the English-speaking countries of Australia, South Africa, the United States, and Canada. Waves of heavy emigration followed the negotiation of independence in 1960 and the Turkish occupation of northern Cyprus in 1974. The population decreased slightly between mid-1974 and 1977 because of emigration, war losses, and a temporary decline in fertility. After 1974 the increase in numbers of Greek Cypriots leaving the island in search of work, especially in the Middle East, contributed to a decline in population, but this tapered off in the 1990s. More than two-thirds of the population is urban.

CHAPTER 2

THE CYPRIOT ECONOMY

Between 1960 and 1973 the Republic of Cyprus, operating a free-enterprise economy based on agriculture and trade, achieved a standard of living higher than most of its neighbours, with the exception of Israel. This progress was substantially assisted by various agencies of the United Nations (UN), operating through the UN Development Program. Generous financial assistance was given by the World Bank and the International Monetary Fund in the form of loans for specific development projects, including electricity supply, port development, and sewerage systems. Individual foreign countries also made some aid available to Cyprus. These countries and organizations provided experts to advise economic planning and initiate productive projects; scholarships and grants provided for the training of Cypriot specialists in these areas. During this time gross domestic product (GDP) and per capita income grew substantially, agricultural production doubled, industrial production and exports of goods and services more than tripled, and tourism became a significant earner of foreign exchange.

EFFECTS OF PARTITION

The Turkish occupation of nearly two-fifths of the country in 1974, involving the displacement of about one-third of the total population, dealt a serious blow to the island's economic development. Greek Cypriot losses of land and personal property in the occupied areas were substantial, and they also lost Famagusta, the only deepwater port, and

FAMAGUSTA

Famagusta, called Gazi Mağusa, in Turkish, is a major port in the Turkish Cypriot-administered portion of northern Cyprus. It lies on the island's east coast in a bay between Capes Greco and Eloea and is about 37 miles (55 km) east of Nicosia. The port possesses the deepest harbour in Cyprus.

Famagusta is a Frankish corruption of its Greek name, *Ammókhostos*, which means "buried in the sand," descriptive of the silted mouth of the Pedieos River north of the town. It was founded as Arsinoe by the Macedonian Egyptian king Ptolemy II (308–246 BCE). An influx of Christian refugees fleeing the downfall of Acre (1291) in Palestine briefly transformed it from a tiny village into one of the richest cities in Christendom. The Lusignan kings of Cyprus were crowned as kings of Jerusalem in Famagusta's 14th-century Gothic-style cathedral of St. Nicholas, which is now a mosque. In 1372 the port was seized by Genoa and in 1489 by Venice. The Venetians made Famagusta the capital of Cyprus and remodeled the town's fortifications. Though ravaged by war and earthquakes, and now only partly inhabited, the old walled and bastioned town contains some of the finest examples of medieval military architecture extant. The walls are 50 feet (15 metres) high and 27 feet (8 metres) thick in places, and north of the well-preserved sea gate (rebuilt 1492) stands the citadel known as Othello's Tower, so called because a lieutenant-governor of Cyprus (1506–08) named Christoforo Moro was allegedly the model for the title character in Shakespeare's play *Othello*. Famagusta fell to the Turks after a bitter and prolonged siege in 1570–71.

The British occupied Cyprus from 1878 to 1960. They built extensive harbour installations at Famagusta, which became a naval base in World War II. During the British administration, a

Othello's Tower, a medieval fortification in Famagusta, Cyprus.
J. Baker—Shostal

modern suburb called Varosha was developed south of Famagusta as a commercial centre and tourist resort. After the Turkish intervention in 1974, Varosha was sealed off to civilians and tourism ceased. Settlers from mainland Turkey were relocated in Famagusta, parts of Varosha (after 1976), and in the surrounding citrus-growing areas. Famagusta is now home to the Eastern Mediterranean University (founded in 1979 as the Institute of Higher Technology; reconstituted and renamed in 1986). Ferry service, begun in 1978 between Mersin, Turkey, and Latakia, Syria, includes Famagusta in its run.

the Nicosia International Airport. GDP of the Greek Cypriot sector dropped by about one-third between 1973 and 1975. Through vigorous efforts, real growth was resumed in the area that remained under the control of the government of the Republic of Cyprus; between 1975 and 1983 the annual rate of growth was estimated to average about 10 percent.

The Turkish-occupied area has not experienced the same prosperity, however, and the Turkish government has had to subsidize its economy. The Turkish area still depends heavily on agriculture. Trade between the two areas ceased in 1974, and the two economies have remained independent. However, the southern zone continues to supply the northern zone with electricity, and the northern zone still processes the sewage of Greek Nicosia.

Since 1983 the economy of the Greek Cypriot sector has flourished, and unemployment and inflation have remained relatively low. Tourism has provided the main leverage of economic growth, and many areas have undergone technological upgrading. In the 1990s the Greek Cypriot sector increasingly transformed itself into a centre of international transit trade, merchant shipping, banking,

and related services. Tourism grew in importance, accounting for between one-tenth and one-fifth of GDP in the first decade of the 21st century. The republic's Greek-run government established special tariff arrangements with the European Union, and from 1990 sought admittance to the organization, whose member countries account for about half of the island's imports. The Greek Cypriot sector joined the EU in 2004 and adopted the euro as its official currency in 2008. Fueled largely by tourism and construction, the economy in the Greek Cypriot sector thrived in the early 21st century (as, generally, did the economy of the Turkish sector); however, it slowed and slid into recession in response to the general economic downturn that began in 2008 in much of the world, and, because of its close association with Greek financial institutions, it remained especially vulnerable to developments in the euro-zone debt crisis that began in 2009.

AGRICULTURE, FORESTRY, AND FISHING

A large portion of the island's arable land is irrigated, mainly in the Mesaoria Plain and around Paphos in the southwest. In response to the often debilitating impact of drought on the agricultural sector, the government has supported the construction of desalination plants. Woodlands and forests occupy about one-fifth of the total land area. Landholdings are generally small, highly fragmented, and dispersed under traditional laws of inheritance. A program of land consolidation was enacted in 1969; it met with resistance, particularly from Turkish Cypriot landowners, and was only very slowly implemented, but it has proceeded with considerable success in the Greek Cypriot sector.

Agricultural production increasingly declined in the first decade of the 21st century, though more rapidly in the Greek sector than in the Turkish sector. The major crops of the Greek Cypriot sector include grapes, deciduous fruits, potatoes, cereal grains, vegetables, olives, and carobs. The area under Turkish occupation produces the bulk of the country's citrus fruits, wheat, barley, carrots, tobacco, and green fodder.

Livestock—especially sheep, goats, pigs, and poultry—and livestock products account for about one-third of the island's total agricultural production. Some cattle are also raised.

Cyprus was once famous for its extensive forests, but the demand for timber for shipbuilding by successive conquerors from the 7th century BCE onward and extensive felling for building and for fuel have cleared most of them. Under the British administration a vigorous policy of conservation and reforestation was pursued, and the Cyprus Forestry College was established at Prodhromos, on the western slopes of Mount Olympus; the Greek Cypriot government continues to operate an ambitious program of forest preservation and development. Forests are found mostly in the mountainous areas and in the Paphos district.

The fishing industry is small, in part because coastal waters are deficient in the nutrients and associated plankton needed to sustain large fish populations. Although the industry has shown some growth in the Greek Cypriot sector, most fish is imported.

RESOURCES AND POWER

Cyprus was for many centuries a noted producer of copper; in Greek the name of the island and the name of the metal are identical. As early as 2500 BCE its mines were being exploited. After other mineral sources were discovered, the mines remained neglected for centuries until they were reopened shortly before World War I. They were subsequently exploited from 1925 until they were closed during the Great Depression of the 1930s. Production resumed after World War II, and copper and other minerals —iron pyrites, asbestos, gypsum, chrome ore—contributed somewhat to external trade; bentonite (a form of clay), umber, and ocher also have been exported. The island's most important copper mines are located in the area of Skouriotissa in the Turkish-occupied zone, though some deposits are found elsewhere. Copper ore reserves have declined substantially, and increasingly the focus is on reprocessing the waste material from previous mining efforts. Extensive quarries for stone and other building materials are for local use.

Cyprus imports all the petroleum needed to power vehicles as well as to generate electricity (which is produced by thermal power stations); however, in the early 21st century there was growing interest in exploring potential gas and petroleum deposits in portions of the Mediterranean within the Cypriot economic zone. The country also continues to be one of the world's major producers of solar energy. Although there are several dams, an adequate water supply remains a constant problem.

MANUFACTURING

Cyprus has limited quantities of raw materials, and this situation restricts the scope for industrial activity. Before the partition of the island, most manufacturing was of goods produced for the domestic market by small owner-operated plants, and a considerable number of those plants were located in the area occupied by the Turks in 1974. Industries in the Republic of Cyprus were subsequently reoriented toward export production, and many factories were built in the south. Petroleum refining, cement manufacturing, and thermal electricity production are the republic's heavy industries, and its light industries produce goods such as cigarettes, beverages, and paper and paper products, as well as some machinery and transport equipment.

FINANCE AND TRADE

The euro is the official currency of the Greek Cypriot sector, and Turkish lira are circulated in the Turkish-occupied area. Financial services have grown in importance since the end of the 20th century, and the banking secrecy practiced in the Greek sector has made it something of a tax haven. Light manufactures —particularly medicine, tobacco products, and prostheses—and foodstuffs constitute the republic's major exports. Petroleum, petroleum products, foodstuffs, and machinery are the chief imports. Historically, chronic trade deficits have been offset by receipts from tourists, remittances sent home by expatriate Greek Cypriots, and receipts from the British military bases on the island. In the Turkish sector industrial products, agricultural products (especially citrus fruits), and minerals are the principal exports; machinery, basic manufactures, and transportation equipment are the major imports.

SERVICES

Tourism became one of the major components of Cyprus's economy after 1960. Most of the tourist accommodations,

LIMASSOL

Limassol is the chief port of the Republic of Cyprus. The city lies on Akrotiri Bay, on the southern coast, southwest of Nicosia; it is the island's second largest city and is also its chief tourist centre.

Limassol's rise from a humble market town between the ancient settlements of Amathus and Curium took place at the end of the Byzantine Empire, when Richard I the Lion-Heart landed there in 1191 and was married to Berengaria of Navarre in the chapel of a castle fortress, now a regional museum and one of only two surviving buildings of the period. After the Genoese seizure of Famagusta in 1372, the port's fortunes increased; but damage from numerous incursions between 1414 and 1426, the Turkish invasion of 1570, and a disastrous earthquake had reduced its population to 150 by 1815. Its resurgence dates from the end of the 19th century, when the island came under British administration.

Limassol's harbour facilities, which were extended in the 1960s to improve its shallow-water location, were increased by a new port (operational in 1974) that was able to provide berthing spaces for large vessels. The Turkish intervention (1974) in northern Cyprus and the closing of the island's main port at Famagusta made Limassol the chief port of the Republic of Cyprus. The port has also taken over much of the trade that once passed through Beirut. In the 1970s and '80s Limassol also became home to many thousands of prosperous Arab refugees from Lebanon and immigrants from Saudi Arabia and Kuwait. Limassol's bustling port exports wines, beverages, fruits, and vegetables. Legumes, vegetables, oranges, lemons, grapefruits, nuts, and apples are grown on the adjacent coastal plain, and goats and cattle are raised as well. The Troodos Mountains lie inland from the plain. Limassol city is linked by roads with Moni, Akrotíri, and Episkopi.

however, were in the portion of the island occupied by the Turks in 1974. After the partition the tourist trade recovered rapidly in the Greek Cypriot sector: to counter the loss of Kyrenia and the Famagusta-Varosha area, which had been the leading seaside resorts, the southern coastal towns of Limassol, Larnaca, and Paphos were further developed to accommodate tourists. Tourism continues to be the largest source of foreign income for the Greek Cypriot sector.

LABOUR AND TAXATION

With the exception of the years immediately following the Turkish invasion, Cyprus has maintained a low overall level of unemployment—among the lowest in Europe—and labour union activity has been strong, with nearly two-thirds of Cypriot workers belonging to unions. Roughly one-fourth of the Cypriot workforce is employed in trade, while the service industry is the second largest employer, with about one-fifth of workers engaged in some service-related occupation, mostly in the tourism sector. Agriculture, once the mainstay of the Cypriot economy, now employs less than one-tenth of the workforce.

Taxation is a major source of state revenue, and the government of the Republic of Cyprus levies direct taxes, including a progressive income tax, and indirect taxes, including various excise taxes and a value-added tax introduced in the mid-1990s.

TRANSPORTATION AND TELECOMMUNICATIONS

In Roman times the island had a well-developed road system, but, by the time of the British occupation in 1878, the only carriage road was between Nicosia and Larnaca. An extensive new road network was built under the British administration. A narrow-gauge public railway proved uneconomical and was closed in the early 1950s, and since then inland travel has been entirely by road. The Greek Cypriot sector continues to develop and maintain an extensive network of modern highways. In 1994 a highway connecting Nicosia, Anthoupolis, and Kokkini Trimithia was completed.

International air services provide connections to all parts of Europe and the Middle East and to some areas of Africa. Nicosia International Airport was closed in 1974, and the airport at Larnaca was developed instead to service the Greek Cypriot sector. An airport at Paphos, also handling international flights, opened in 1983. Flights to the Turkish-occupied sector arrive from or through Turkey and use an airport at Gečitkale (Lefkoniko).

There is no significant coastal shipping, and much of the merchant marine registered to Cyprus is foreign-owned. The great bulk of the island's international trade remains seaborne, and the main ports of the Greek Cypriot sector, Limassol and Larnaca, are thoroughly modernized; Vasilikos is a major industrial port. Turkish shipping uses Famagusta.

The Greek Cypriot sector became a major international telecommunications hub in the 1990s, installing submarine fibre-optic cables and satellite linkup facilities.

CHAPTER 3

CYPRIOT GOVERNMENT AND SOCIETY

The constitution of the Republic of Cyprus, adopted in 1960, provided that executive power be exercised by a Greek Cypriot president and a Turkish Cypriot vice president, elected to five-year terms by universal suffrage, and that there be a Council of Ministers (cabinet) comprising seven Greek Cypriot and three Turkish Cypriot members. It also called for an elected House of Representatives with 50 seats, divided between Greek and Turkish Cypriots in the proportion of 35 to 15 and elected for terms of five years.

The constitution, derived from the negotiations in Zürich, Switzerland, in 1959 between representatives of the governments of Greece and Turkey, was not widely accepted by the citizens of the new republic. The Greek Cypriots, whose struggle against the British had been for *enosis* (union with Greece) and not for independence, regretted the failure to achieve this national aspiration. As a result, it was not long after the establishment of the republic that the Greek Cypriot majority began to regard many of the provisions, particularly those relating to finance and to local government, as unworkable. Proposals for amendments were rejected by the Turkish government, and, after the outbreak of fighting between the two Cypriot communities in late 1963, the constitution was suspended. In the Republic of Cyprus after the Turkish occupation of 1974, the constitution's provisions remained in force where practicable; the main formal change has been the increase in the number of seats in the House of Representatives to 80, although the 24 seats allocated to Turks have remained vacant.

On the Turkish side of the demarcation line, there have been, since 1974, a popularly elected president, prime minister, and legislative assembly, all serving five-year terms of office. A new constitution was approved for the Turkish Republic of Northern Cyprus (TRNC) by its electorate in 1985.

Local government in the Republic of Cyprus is at the district, municipal, rural municipality, and village levels. District officers are appointed by the government; local councils are elected, as are the mayors of municipalities.

JUSTICE

The legal code of Cyprus is based on Roman law. In the Greek Cypriot zone judges are appointed by the government, but the judiciary is entirely independent of the executive power. The Supreme Court is the highest court and also serves as the final appeals court in the republic.

A Permanent Assize Court has criminal jurisdiction over the whole island, and district courts handle criminal, civil, and admiralty matters. The Turkish Cypriot zone has a similar system of justice.

POLITICAL PROCESS

The oldest established political party in the Republic of Cyprus is the Progressive Party of the Working People (Anorthotiko Komma Ergazomenou Laou; AKEL), founded in 1941. A pro-Moscow communist party that controlled the principal trade union federation, it received about one-third of the vote in the first 25 years of the Republic of Cyprus. Following the collapse of communism in Russia and eastern Europe, AKEL lost much of its support, with some reformists breaking away to form their own party. Other parties have had varying success. Among them are the Movement of Social Democrats EDEK (Kinima Sosialdimokraton EDEK)

DIMITRIS CHRISTOFIAS

Dimitris Christofias (born August 29, 1946 Kato Dhikomo, Cyprus) was sworn in as president of the Republic of Cyprus, the Greek portion of the divided island, on February 28, 2008. The victory received worldwide attention because the new leader was Greek Cyprus's first president from AKEL, the Marxist-Leninist-oriented Progressive Party of the Working People. Speculation was rife as to what path his leadership would take. In the years before the election, Christofias was seen as something of a euroskeptic, and his party had urged delay in converting the country's currency from the Cyprus pound to the euro (a conversion that occurred on January 1, 2008). He was also a critic of the U.S.-led Iraq war and of the British military bases on Cyprus. In his inaugural address, however, Christofias stressed his commitment to previous agreements, including those with the EU and the UN. He declared that his two main priorities would be finding a solution to the problem of a divided Cyprus and building a fairer society.

and the Democratic Rally (Dimokratikos Synagermos). In the Turkish Cypriot zone the major parties include the National Unity Party (Ulusal Birlik Partisi), the Communal Democracy Party (Toplumcu Demokrasi Partisi), the Republican Turkish Party (Cumhuriyetc̦i Türk Partisi), and the Democrat Party (Demokrat Parti).

SECURITY

The island of Cyprus is home to a complicated mixture of military forces. The Republic of Cyprus has a small national guard consisting of volunteers and conscripts, and men between the ages of 18 and 50 are required to serve up to 26 months in the military. The army of the TRNC requires 24 months of military service from men within that same age-group. Likewise, both sides maintain close military ties with their respective kinsmen on the mainland; the Republic of Cyprus's national guard has a large number of officers from the Greek army, and Turkey maintains a large garrison in northern Cyprus. In addition, because of the continued tensions between the two sides—which occasionally have flared into violence—the UN has maintained peacekeeping troops in Cyprus (UNFICYP) who police the demilitarized zone that divides the country; the United Kingdom also maintains two sovereign military bases in Cyprus.

HEALTH

Health standards in Cyprus are high because of a favourable climate and well-organized public and private health services. Since the eradication of malaria shortly after World War II and, later, that of echinococcosis (hydatid disease), the island has been free from major diseases. Life expectancy is about 78 years for men and 82 years for women, higher than the EU average for men and about the same as the EU average for women. The infant mortality rate is higher than the EU average.

HOUSING

Housing became a major preoccupation of the Republic of Cyprus following the Turkish invasion of 1974 and the subsequent displacement and relocation

Modern housing in Nicosia, Cyprus. Georg Gerster—Rapho /Photo Researchers

of Greek Cypriots to the south of the country. The government engaged in a long-term program to stimulate the construction of low-cost housing, provided low-interest loans for home buyers, and temporarily housed refugees in homes abandoned by Turkish Cypriots who fled to the north during the war. The government has continued to provide rent subsidies for thousands of refugee families and has also provided housing assistance for other low-income families.

EDUCATION

In the Greek Cypriot sector, 12 grades of free education are provided for children beginning at age 5; schooling is compulsory through age 15. The last three years may be taken at a technical or vocational school or at a lyceum, the latter offering courses stressing such fields as classical studies, the sciences, or economics. Postsecondary facilities include schools for teacher training, technical instruction, hospitality training, tourism guides, nursing, public health, and police work. Greek Cypriots opened the University of Cyprus in 1992; many students, however, attend universities abroad, especially in Greece, Britain, or the United States.

The education system in the Turkish sector is administered separately, and the Turkish Cypriots maintain an excellent public-school system with facilities similar to those in the Greek sector and several institutions of specialized postsecondary education. As in the Greek sector, many Turkish Cypriots travel abroad (most to Turkey) for postsecondary education. The fine educational opportunities provided by both the Greek and the Turkish administrations have not been without drawbacks, as many of the most qualified Cypriot graduates—both Greek and Turkish—seek employment abroad.

CHAPTER 4

CYPRIOT CULTURAL LIFE

The culture of Cyprus is divided between the northern Turkish and the southern Greek sections of the country. Since 1974 the Turkish community in northern Cyprus has promoted its own Turkish and Islamic culture, supporting its own newspapers and periodicals and changing many place-names to Turkish. The anniversary of the proclamation of the TRNC (November 15) is celebrated in the north, as are traditional Muslim holidays.

Greek Cypriots speak a dialect of Greek and maintain a somewhat ambivalent attitude about mainland Greeks. However, most Greek Cypriots who go abroad for their postsecondary education travel to Greece, and these young people share in the popular culture of Greece, which is itself increasingly cosmopolitan. Even so, Greek Cypriots take care to preserve their traditional culture and to observe such important holidays as Easter (and the pre-Easter Carnival) and Anthestiria, a spring flower festival.

Despite years of civil conflict in the 1950s, '60s, and '70s, the younger generation of Greek Cypriots has grown up in a relatively peaceful, settled, and prosperous society that encompasses aspects of traditional culture while welcoming world trends in dress and entertainment. These trends were introduced not only by the mass media but also by a tremendous influx of young travelers, whose presence can be felt in the dance clubs and bars that now abound throughout the island.

Greek and Turkish Cypriots alike enjoy a rich tradition of handicrafts and folk art. Among the best-known expressions of this art internationally are Cypriot lacework—particularly that produced in the town of Lefkara near Nicosia—and silversmithing, which is practiced throughout the island.

Geography has left Cyprus heir to numerous culinary traditions—particularly those of the Levant, Anatolia, and Greece—but some dishes, such as the island's halloumi cheese, pourgouri (a dish of boiled cracked wheat), hiromeri (a pressed, smoked, and aged leg of pork), and sucuk (a confection made of thickened grape juice and almonds), are purely Cypriot. As in much of the Mediterranean world, the appetizer, or meze, in Cyprus plays a central role, often taking the place of the entrée. Fresh fruits and vegetables are a part of every meal, and Cyprus has long been famous for its wine, viticulture having been practiced on the island for thousands of years.

THE ARTS

Cyprus has figured in the literature of Europe for thousands of years, from

Closeup of the hands of a lacemaker plying her trade on the island of Cyprus. Cris Haigh/Stone/ Getty Images.

the works of Ionic lyric poets to modern travel memoirs such as Lawrence Durrell's *Bitter Lemons* (1957). Literary traditions are strong on the island itself. Drawing on oral tradition, on classical forms—such as the tekerleme (rigmarole) and mani (quatrain)—and on contemporary styles, Turkish Cypriot singers such as Acar Akalın and Neşe Yaşin have developed a body of work that is well known on the Turkish mainland though largely untranslated into other languages. Contemporary Greek Cypriot poets are somewhat better known beyond the island, having been translated into other European languages. Several literary journals are published, and small presses issue hundreds of books in Greek and Turkish each year. Poetry is also an important element in the growing "peace culture" movement, which seeks to forge social and cultural links across the island's ethnic divide. Numerous painters and sculptors work in Cyprus as well.

The Cultural Services office keeps the state's collection of modern Cypriot art on permanent exhibition, and also sponsors the annual Kypria International Festival of music and theatrical performances. In the village of Lemba, near Paphos, the Cyprus College of Art runs courses for postgraduate art students. The government encourages young composers, musicians, and folk dance groups. Both the Turkish and the Greek Cypriot communities have active film industries, and Cypriot motion pictures have received a number of awards in international competitions. Classical and folk music enjoy a wide following among Cypriots of all ages, and the respective folk music traditions of the Greek and Turkish communities, combined with international styles, have contributed to the development of native Greek Cypriot and Turkish Cypriot popular music styles.

CULTURAL INSTITUTIONS

The ancient cultural traditions of Cyprus are maintained partly by private enterprise and partly by government sponsorship, especially through the Cultural Services office of the Republic of Cyprus's Ministry of Education and Culture, which publishes books, awards prizes for literature, and promotes Cypriot publications. Cities have public libraries, as do many rural communities. The government-sponsored Cyprus Theatre Organization stages plays by contemporary Cypriot dramatists as well as classical works. The ancient theatres of Salamis and Soli in the Turkish sector and Kourion (Curium) in the Greek portion have been restored; a variety of plays are staged at Kourion, and a Greek theatre has been built at Nicosia.

Many noteworthy buildings survive from the Lusignan and Venetian periods, in particular the Gothic cathedrals at Nicosia and Famagusta and the Abbey of Bellapais near Kyrenia. There are other Gothic churches throughout the island. Orthodox Christians also built numerous

A view of Kantara Castle in the northern portion of Cyprus. The castle is one of three "crusader castles" built to protect the island during the Crusades. Michael Runkel/Robert Harding World Imagery/Getty Images

churches in a distinctive style that was often influenced by the Gothic; the interiors of these illustrate the continued development of Byzantine art. Cyprus has notable examples of medieval and Renaissance military architecture, such as the castles of Kyrenia, St. Hilarion, Buffavento, and Kantara and the elaborate Venetian fortifications of Nicosia and Famagusta.

Additional sites of cultural significance include the town of Paphos, held to be the legendary birthplace of Aphrodite, which houses a temple constructed in her honour dating from the 12th century BCE; the painted churches of the Troodos region, a complex of Byzantine churches and monasteries renowned for their display of murals in Byzantine and post-Byzantine styles; and the Neolithic settlements at Choirokotia, inhabited from the 7th to the 4th millennium BCE. These sites were designated UNESCO World Heritage sites in 1980, 1985, and 1998, respectively.

OLD AND NEW PAPHOS

Old Paphos, which was settled by Greek colonists in about the 10th century BCE, contained a famous temple of Aphrodite and was the legendary site where that goddess was said to have been born from the sea foam. In Hellenic times Paphos was second only to Salamis in extent and influence among the states of Cyprus. The Cinyrad dynasty ruled Paphos until its final conquest by Ptolemy I of Egypt (294 BCE). Old Paphos dwindled in influence after the fall of the Cinyradae, the foundation of New Paphos, and the Roman conquest of Cyprus (58 BCE). It was finally deserted after the 4th century CE.

New Paphos, which had been the port town of Old Paphos, became the administrative capital of the whole island in Ptolemaic and Roman times. The city was attacked and destroyed by Muslim raiders in 960 CE. The modern town began to grow only after the British occupation in 1878. The harbour, which was the centre of the city's life, was improved in 1908 and 1959 but remains too small to handle large commercial traffic and thus serves only an active local fishing fleet. Despite economic difficulties arising from the settlement in Paphos of some 5,000 Greek Cypriot refugees after the Turkish occupation of 1974, by the end of that decade the city had become the focus of strong economic development, including an industrial estate and tourist hotels. The city's manufacturing consists of small enterprises producing clothing, footwear, canned meat, beverages, and vegetable oils. Local points of interest include Orthodox churches, the Djami Kebir Mosque, Paphos Castle, and Frankish baths.

SPORTS AND RECREATION

Sports play a major role in the Greek Cypriot community, as they have since Classical times, when stadiums stood at the heart of the island's chief cities. Through the Cyprus Sports Organization, an official body formed in 1969, the government has built stadiums, sports halls, and swimming pools and has subsidized associations and clubs for a wide spectrum of sports; there are a professional football (soccer) league and a semiprofessional basketball league.

Cypriot athletes began to compete in the Olympic Games in 1924 but as members of the Greek national team. In 1978 the Cyprus National Olympic Committee was admitted to the International Olympic Committee, and the Republic of Cyprus has been sending its own national team—consisting of athletes from the Greek Cypriot sector only—to the Games since 1980. There have been unsuccessful attempts at athletic cooperation or contests between the Turkish and Greek communities, and international sports-governing bodies have not recognized the sports associations in the Turkish sector of Cyprus.

MEDIA AND PUBLISHING

Television and radio are controlled in the Greek sector by the semigovernmental Cyprus Broadcasting Corporation and are financed by government subsidies, taxes, and advertising. Throughout the island, broadcasts are in Greek, Turkish, English, and Armenian, and daily and weekly newspapers are published in Greek, Turkish, and English. The Turkish sector receives broadcasts from Turkey.

CHAPTER 5

CYPRUS: PAST AND PRESENT

Tools and other artifacts provide the earliest evidence of human activity on Cyprus; artifacts and burned animal bones found at Aetokremnos on the southern coast have been dated to about 12,000 years ago. Whether these finds indicate a permanent human occupation of the island or intermittent visits by seafaring hunter-gatherers remains a source of debate. The first known settlement, dated as early as 9,000 years ago, was at Khirokitia (near the southern coast), a town of about 2,000 inhabitants who lived in well-built two-story round stone houses. The presence of small quantities of obsidian, a type of volcanic rock not native to the island, is the only sign of the island's contact with other cultures. Khirokitia and several smaller associated settlements disappeared after a few centuries, leaving the island uninhabited for nearly 2,000 years. The beginning of the next period of habitation dates to 4500–4000 BCE; the sites of small villages from that time have been excavated north of Kourion at Sotira near the southern coast and also in the Kyrenia Mountains, and ornaments of picrolite (a variety of soapstone) and copper have also been found in those areas.

THE BRONZE AGE

The Chalcolithic Period (Copper Age), which dates from 3000 to 2500 BCE, was followed by the Bronze Age. Several styles of well-made decorative pottery from the Middle

IDALIUM

Idalium was an ancient city in southern Cyprus, near the modern village of Dali. Of pre-Greek origin, Idalium was one of 10 Cypriot kingdoms listed on the prism (many-sided tablet) of the Assyrian king Esarhaddon (680–669 BCE). Eventually dominated by the Phoenician city of Citium, it became the centre of a cult of Aphrodite and of the Greco-Phoenician deity Resheph-Apollo. A terra-cotta model found there (now in the Louvre) is believed to represent the Resheph-Apollo temple.

Bronze Age (1900–1600 BCE) demonstrate advanced craftsmanship, and imports from Crete, Anatolia, Syria, and Egypt prove that external trade had begun by this time. It is possible that the name Alashiya or Alasia, both of which occur in Hittite and Egyptian records in connection with the supply of copper, refers to Cyprus. These trade links probably accounted for the foundation of new settlements in the eastern part of the island that became international trading centres.

The Late Bronze Age (1600–1050 BCE) was one of the most formative periods of the life of ancient Cyprus. The island's international contacts extended from the Aegean Sea to the Levant and the Nile River delta. (Thutmose III of Egypt claimed Cyprus as one of his conquests about 1500 BCE.) Writing, in the form of a linear script known as Cypro-Minoan, was borrowed from Crete. Cypriot craftsmen were distinguished for fine jewelry, ivory carving, and bronze figures. From about 1400 BCE Mycenaean pottery was imported from mainland Greece, and

it is possible that Mycenaean artists accompanied the merchants. There is evidence of Greek immigration from the Peloponnese after 1200 BCE, with the collapse of Mycenaean civilization. West of Famagusta was Engomi, the principal city and port; its massive city walls and houses of hewn stone demonstrate a high level of prosperity.

GREEK IMMIGRATION

The immigration of settlers from Greece, which had begun at least by 1200 BCE, led to the foundation of Greek kingdoms covering most of the island, and, since the start of the 1st millennium BCE, the Greek language has been predominant in Cyprus; the fact that the dialectal form in which it first appears is known as Arcado-Cypriot confirms traditions of the Peloponnesian origin—and specifically of the Arcadian origin—of the immigrants. They founded new cities, which became the capitals of six ancient Greek kingdoms on Cyprus: Curium (Greek: Kourion), Paphos, Marion, Soli (Greek: Soloi), Lapithos, and Salamis.

SALAMIS

Salamis, one of the principal cities of ancient Cyprus, was located on the east coast of the island, north of modern Famagusta. According to the Homeric epics, Salamis was founded after the Trojan War by the archer Teucer, who came from the island of Salamis, off Attica. This literary tradition probably reflects the Sea Peoples' occupation of Cyprus (C. 1193 BCE), Teucer perhaps representing Tjekker of the Egyptian records. Later, the city grew because of its excellent harbour; it became the chief Cypriot outlet for trade with Phoenicia, Egypt, and Cilicia.

Salamis came under Persian control in 525 bce. In 306 BCE Demetrius I Poliorcetes of Macedonia won a great naval victory there over Ptolemy I of Egypt. Salamis was sacked in the Jewish revolt of 115–117 CE and suffered repeatedly from earthquakes; it was completely rebuilt by the Christian emperor Constantius II (reigned 337–361 CE) and given the name Constantia. Under Christian rule, Salamis was the metropolitan see of Cyprus. Destroyed again by the Arabs under Muʿāwiyah (C. 648), the city was thereafter abandoned.

About 800 BCE a Phoenician colony was founded at Citium (Greek: Kition), near modern Larnaca, as a dependency of the mother city, Tyre. A seventh kingdom, Amathus, remained for some time under the control of the earlier indigenous inhabitants; the language used there was called Eteo-Cypriot ("True Cypriot") by the Greeks. Amathus became active politically, especially in external trade relations. Spectacular chariot burials of the royal family of Salamis—which closely match descriptions found in the Homeric poems, suggesting inspiration by them—are evidence of an advancing civilization in the late Iron Age.

ASSYRIAN AND EGYPTIAN DOMINATION

In 709 BCE Sargon II of Assyria erected a stela at Citium recording the fact that seven Cypriot kings had paid him homage; subsequent Assyrian documents mention 11 tributary kingdoms: the seven already cited plus Citium, Kyrenia, Tamassos, and Idalium. This subordination to Assyria, probably rather nominal, lasted until about 663. For the next hundred years, Cyprus enjoyed a period of complete independence and massive development. Epic poetry grew increasingly popular, and much was written on the island; Stasinus of Cyprus, credited with the authorship of the lost epic poem *Cypria*, was highly regarded among the poets of this literary style in the 7th century. Bronze, iron, delicate jewelry, and ivory work are characteristic of this period; notable examples are the ivory throne and bedstead excavated from a royal tomb at Salamis dating from about 700 BCE.

An ivory sphinx found in a tomb at Salamis. DEA/G. Dagli Orti/De Agostini/Getty Images.

When the Assyrian empire finally broke up at the end of the 7th century BCE, Egypt, under the Saite dynasty, became the predominant power in the eastern Mediterranean. About 569 the Cypriot kingdoms recognized the

CYPRIOT SYLLABARY

The Cypriot syllabary, used on the island chiefly from the 6th to the 3rd century BCE, consists of 56 signs, each of which represents a different syllable. Most inscriptions written with this syllabary are in the Greek language, although the syllabary was originally designed for writing the earlier non-Greek language of Cyprus. The Cypriot syllabary was eventually replaced by the Greek alphabet as part of Alexander the Great's program of Hellenization. The classical Cypriot syllabary is apparently a late development of the still undeciphered Cypro-Minoan script (containing 63 syllabic symbols), which was found on a number of clay tablets from Cyprus and Syria and dates from about 1500 to about 1100 BCE. The Cypro-Minoan script in turn is thought to be a distant offshoot of the early Cretan scripts (Linear A and Linear B).

pharaoh Ahmose II as their overlord. Direct Egyptian influence was not always apparent, but many limestone sculptures reproduced Egyptian conventions in dress, and some statues were directly inspired by Egyptian models. A more important influence in the late Archaic period (750–475 BCE) came from the artistic schools of Ionia, which was also probably the same source of the inspiration for issuing coinage; the first Cypriot coins were circulated for King Euelthon of Salamis in 560–525 BCE.

THE PERSIAN EMPIRE

In 525 BCE the Cypriot kings transferred their allegiance to the Achaemenid (Persian) conquerors of Egypt. The Cypriots retained their independence until the accession of Darius I in 522 but were then incorporated into the fifth satrapy of the Persian empire. When the Ionians revolted in 499, all the kingdoms of Cyprus except Amathus joined them; the revolt was subsequently suppressed, culminating in sieges of Paphos and Soli. During Xerxes I's invasion of Greece in 480 BCE, the Cypriot kings, like the Ionians, contributed naval contingents to his forces. Cyprus remained under Persian rule during the 5th century in spite of a major Athenian expedition there in about 450. Evagoras, who became king of Salamis in 411 BCE, maintained a pro-Hellenic policy—with some help from Athens—and succeeded in extending his rule over a large portion of the island. He was defeated by the Persians in 381 and was assassinated three years later. After the victory of Alexander the Great over the last Achaemenid ruler, Darius III, at Issus in 333 BCE, the Cypriot kings rallied to Alexander and assisted him at the siege of Tyre. During the Classical period (475–325 BCE), Cypriot art came under strong Attic influence.

EVAGORAS

Evagoras, king of Salamis (C. 410–374 BCE), maintained a policy of friendship with Athens and promoted Hellenism in Cyprus; he eventually fell under Persian domination.

Most of what is known of him is found in the panegyric "Evagoras" by Isocrates, where he is described, with extravagant praise, as a model ruler whose aim was to promote the welfare of his state by cultivation of Greek refinement and civilization. Evagoras' services to Athens were recognized by the gift of Athenian citizenship. For a time he also maintained friendly relations with Achaemenian Persia, securing Persian support for Athens in the early years of the Corinthian War (395–387) against Sparta. He participated, along with the Persian fleet, in the naval victory over Sparta off Cnidus (394), but from 391 Evagoras and the Persians were virtually at war. Aided by the Athenians and the Egyptians, Evagoras extended his rule over the greater part of Cyprus and to several cities of Anatolia. When Athens withdrew its support after the peace of Antalcides (386), Evagoras' troops fought without allies until they were crushed at Citium (Larnaca, Cyprus) in 381. He fled to Salamis, where he managed to conclude a peace that allowed him to remain nominally king of Salamis, though in reality he was a vassal of the Achaemenian king. He was assassinated by a eunuch.

HELLENISTIC AND ROMAN RULE

Alexander allowed the Cypriot kingdoms to continue but took from them the right to issue coinage. After his death in 323 BCE, his successors fought for control of Cyprus. The eventual victor was Ptolemy I of Egypt, who suppressed the kingdoms and made the island a province of his Egyptian kingdom. He forced the last king of Salamis, Nicocreon, to commit suicide in 310 BCE, together with all his family. For two and a half centuries, Cyprus remained a Ptolemaic possession, ruled by a strategus, or governor-general.

CYPRUS AS A ROMAN PROVINCE

Cyprus was annexed by the Roman Republic in 58 BCE and, along with Cilicia on the coast of Anatolia, was made into a Roman province. One of its first proconsuls was the orator and writer Cicero. Cyprus was briefly ceded to Cleopatra VII of Egypt by Julius Caesar, and this status was confirmed by Mark Antony, but, after the victory of Caesar's heir, Octavian (subsequently the emperor Augustus), over Mark Antony and Cleopatra at Actium in 31 BCE, it became a Roman possession again. Cyprus was originally administered as part of the "imperial" province of Syria but became a separate "senatorial" province in 22 BCE. Its governors resumed the old republican title of proconsul, although there is evidence that Augustus did influence the Senate's choice. For the next 600 years, Cyprus enjoyed peace, disturbed only by occasional earthquakes and epidemics and by a Jewish uprising suppressed by a

SAINT BARNABAS

Barnabas was a hellenized Jew who joined the Jerusalem church soon after Christ's crucifixion, sold his property, and gave the proceeds to the community (Acts 4:36–37). He was one of the Cypriots who founded (Acts 11:19–20) the church in Antioch, where he preached. After he called Paul from Tarsus as his assistant (Acts 11:25), they undertook joint missionary activity (Acts 13–14) and then went to Jerusalem in 48. Shortly afterward, a serious conflict separated them, and Barnabas sailed to Cyprus (Acts 15:39). There is no contemporary mention of his subsequent activity, except for a brief reference by Paul a few years later (I Corinthians 9:6).

Nothing is known for certain about the time or circumstances of his death. Barnabas's alleged martyrdom and burial in Cyprus are described in the apocryphal *Journeys and Martyrdom of Barnabas*, a 5th-century forgery. Subsequent church tradition finds Barnabas in Alexandria, Egypt, and ascribes to him the *Letter of Barnabas* (an exegetical treatise on the use of the Old Testament) or pictures him in Rome and assumes that he wrote the *Letters to the Hebrews*. Barnabas's reputed tomb, discovered in 488, is near the Monastery of St. Barnabas, in the Cypriot city of Salamis, whose Christian community was founded by Paul and Barnabas. The feast day of Barnabas is observed on June 11.

lieutenant of the future emperor Hadrian in 116 CE. Many large public buildings were erected, among them a gymnasium and theatre at Salamis, a theatre at Kourion, and the governor's palace at Paphos.

EARLY CHRISTIANITY

One of the most important events in the Roman period was the introduction of Christianity to Cyprus. The apostle Paul, accompanied by Barnabas (later St. Barnabas), a native of the Cypriot Jewish community, preached there about 45 CE and converted the proconsul, Sergius Paulus. By the time of Constantine I the Great, Christians were numerous on the island and may have constituted a majority of the population.

BYZANTINE EMPIRE

After the division of the Roman Empire in 395, Cyprus remained subject to the Eastern, or Byzantine, Empire at Constantinople, being part of the diocese of the Orient governed from Antioch. In ecclesiastical matters, however, the Church of Cyprus was autocephalous—i.e., independent of the Patriarchate of Antioch—having been given that privilege in 488 by the emperor Zeno. The archbishop received the rights, still valued and practiced today, to carry a sceptre instead of a crosier and to sign his name in purple ink, the imperial colour.

There was a break in direct rule from Constantinople in 688 when Justinian II and the caliph ʿAbd al-Malik signed an unusual treaty neutralizing the island,

Fresco of the Virgin Mary and the Christ child, flanked by angels, on the walls of the Byzantine church of Panagia tis Asinou on Cyprus. The church is famous for its artwork. DEA/A. Dagli Orti/De Agostini/Getty Images.

which had been subject to Arab raids. For almost 300 years Cyprus was a kind of condominium (joint dominion) of the Byzantine Empire and the Caliphate, and, although the treaty was frequently violated by both sides, the arrangement lasted until 965, when the emperor Nicephorus II

Phocas gained Cyprus completely for the Byzantines. The period that followed was one of modest prosperity.

A remarkable mosaic of the 6th century, at Kiti, is the best example of Eastern Roman art of that date, comparable to works at Ravenna, Italy. Another equally remarkable mosaic of roughly the same date, at Lythrangomi, was destroyed in 1974. Wall paintings demonstrate close contact with Constantinople; those at Asinou, in particular, are noteworthy as being the earliest of an unparalleled series of mural paintings showing successive developments of Byzantine art.

About 1185 a Byzantine governor of Cyprus, Isaac Comnenus, rebelled and proclaimed himself emperor. Isaac resisted attacks from the Byzantine emperors Andronicus I Comnenus and Isaac II Angelus, but in 1191, on engaging in hostilities with an English Crusader fleet under King Richard I (the Lion-Heart), he was defeated and imprisoned. The island was seized by Richard, from whom it was acquired by the Crusading order of the Knights Templar; because they were unable to pay his price, he took it back and sold it to Guy of Lusignan, the dispossessed king of Jerusalem.

THE LUSIGNAN KINGDOM AND GENOESE AND VENETIAN RULE

Guy, a Frenchman who called himself lord of Cyprus, invited families that had lost their lands in Palestine after the fall of Jerusalem to the Muslims under Saladin to settle in Cyprus and thereby laid the basis for a feudal monarchy that survived to the end of the Middle Ages. His brother and successor, Amalric, obtained the title of king from the Holy Roman emperor Henry VI. The earliest kings of the Lusignan dynasty were involved in the affairs of the small territory still left to

the kingdom of Jerusalem, and this commitment drained the resources of Cyprus until the kingdom collapsed in 1291 with the fall of Acre. Over the next hundred years, Cyprus gained a reputation in Europe for having immense riches, especially among its nobles and Famagustan merchants. Famagusta's wealth derived from its position as the last entrepôt for European trade adjacent to the Levant.

The kings of Cyprus had kept alive the Crusading idea, and the island remained a base for counterattacks against the Muslims. In 1361 the Cypriot king Peter I devoted himself to organizing a Crusade; he captured Adalia (Antalya) on the Cilician coast of Anatolia, and in 1365, after having collected money and mercenaries in western Europe, he seized and sacked Alexandria. He was not able to maintain the conquest, however, and was soon forced to abandon Alexandria. At his son's accession the rivalry between Genoa and Venice over control of Cyprus's valuable trade resulted in Genoa's taking possession of Famagusta and holding on to it for nearly a century, which thus led to a rapid decline in the island's prosperity. In 1426 an expedition from Egypt raided and overran the island, which from then on paid tribute to Cairo. The last Lusignan king, James II, seized the throne with the help of an Egyptian force and in 1464 expelled the Genoese from Famagusta. He married a Venetian noblewoman, Caterina Cornaro, and, on his death (which was followed by that of his posthumous son), she succeeded him as the last monarch of Cyprus. During

CATERINA CORNARO

Caterina Cornaro (born 1454, Venice, Venetian republic [Italy]—died July 10, 1510, Venice) was a Venetian noblewoman who became queen of Cyprus by marrying James II, king of Cyprus, Jerusalem, and Armenia, thereby supplying him with a much-needed alliance with Venice.

The marriage agreement was reached in 1468, but in the next four years James considered other possible alliances by way of marriage, especially with Naples. In 1472, Caterina finally departed for Cyprus, where the formal ceremony took place. James died in 1473, leaving her and her unborn child heirs to the kingdom. Unsuccessful plotters against James now conspired to deprive Caterina of the throne; and when she bore a son, James III (August 1473), Cyprus was seized by the archbishop of Nicosia and his Neapolitan allies. Imprisoned briefly, Caterina was restored by the intervention of Venice.

The early death of Caterina's son (1474) precipitated further conspiracies, all of which were foiled by the Venetians, who gradually usurped Caterina's power and finally forced the queen to abdicate (1489). She was received with honour at Venice and given the castle and town of Asolo, which she governed beneficently. She died after having fled Asolo when her castle was occupied by imperial troops.

her reign she was under strong Venetian pressure and was eventually persuaded to cede Cyprus to the Republic of Venice. It remained a Venetian possession for 82 years, until its capture by the Ottomans.

OTTOMAN RULE

A Turkish invading force landed in Cyprus in 1570 and seized Nicosia; the following year Famagusta fell after a long siege, which ushered in the beginning of more than three centuries of Ottoman rule. The Latin church was suppressed and the Orthodox hierarchy restored; after feudal tenure was abolished, the Greek peasantry acquired inalienable and hereditary rights to land. Taxes were at first reduced but later greatly increased and arbitrarily raised. In the 18th century the Orthodox archbishop was made responsible for tax collection.

Thousands of Muslims were settled on the island immediately following the Ottoman conquest. To the sultans Cyprus was an unimportant province; its governors were indolent, inefficient, somewhat oppressive, and corrupt. There were Turkish uprisings in 1764 and 1833, and in 1821 the Orthodox archbishop was hanged on suspicion of sympathy with the rebels in mainland Greece. The sultanate's various imperial proclamations in the 19th century promising reform had no effect in Cyprus, where local opposition blocked them.

BRITISH RULE

The Cyprus Convention of 1878 between Britain and Turkey provided that Cyprus, while remaining under Turkish sovereignty, should be administered by the British government. Britain's aim in occupying Cyprus was to secure a base in the eastern Mediterranean for possible operations in the Caucasus or Mesopotamia as part of the British guarantee to secure the sultan's Asian possessions from Russia. In 1914, when Britain and Turkey became adversaries during World War I, the former annexed the island; Turkey recognized this under the Treaty of Lausanne in 1923. Two years later Cyprus was officially declared a crown colony.

British occupation was initially welcomed by the Greek population, which from the start expected the British to transfer Cyprus to Greece. The Greek Cypriots' demand for enosis (union with Greece) was opposed by Turkish Cypriots, constituting a major division in the island's politics; a string of almost annual petitions demanding enosis were matched by counterpetitions and demonstrations from the Turkish Cypriots. Britain had made an offer to transfer the island in 1915, on condition that Greece fulfill its treaty obligations toward Serbia when that country was attacked by Bulgaria; the Greek government refused it, and the offer was not renewed. In 1931 the demand for enosis led to riots in Nicosia.

Cyprus was untouched by World War II, apart from a few air raids. In 1947 the governor, in accordance with the British Labour Party's declaration on colonial policy, published proposals for greater self-government. They were rejected in favour of the slogan "enosis and only enosis." In 1955 Lieutenant Colonel Georgios Grivas (known as Dighenis), a Cypriot who had served as an officer in the Greek army, began a concerted campaign for enosis. His National Organization of Cypriot Struggle (Ethnikí Orgánosis Kipriakoú Agónos; EOKA) bombed public buildings and attacked and killed both Greek Cypriot and British opponents of enosis. British jurist Lord Radcliffe, among others, suggested self-government in 1956, but all of the proposals were rejected, and the attacks continued. Archbishop Makarios III, who as ethnarch considered it his duty to champion the national aspirations of the Greek Cypriots, was deported to the Seychelles. He was released from exile in March 1957 and soon made his headquarters in Athens. By that time the operations of EOKA had been reduced, but on the other hand the Turkish Cypriot minority, led by Fazıl Küçük, expressed alarm and demanded either retrocession to Turkey or partition. Public opinion in Greece and Turkey rallied in support of the two communities, respectively; riots ensued, and Greek residents were expelled from Turkey. Despite mediation by the United Nations, the two sides reached no solution.

The Greek and Turkish governments took a decisive step in February 1959, when they reached an agreement in Zürich. Later that same month, at a conference in London, the British government and representatives of the Greek Cypriot and Turkish Cypriot communities

Archbishop Makarios III, who was exiled to the Seychelles in 1956 because of his support for enosis, or Cypriot unification with Greece. Makarios was elected president of the newly independent Cyprian republic in 1959. Popperfoto/Getty Images.

accepted the Greek-Turkish compromise. In 1960 treaties that made Cyprus an independent republic, with Britain retaining sovereignty over military bases at Akrotiri and Dhekélia, were ratified in Nicosia. According to the terms of the treaties, the new republic would not participate in a political or economic union with any other state, nor would it be subject to partition. Greece, Turkey, and Britain guaranteed the independence, integrity, and security of the republic, and Greece and Turkey agreed to respect the integrity of the areas remaining under British sovereignty. In December 1959 Makarios was elected president and Küçük vice president, both of whom could exercise a veto in matters relating to security, defense, and foreign affairs. Turkish Cypriots, who made up less than one-fifth of the population, were to represent three-tenths of the civil service and two-fifths of the army and to elect three-tenths of the House of Representatives, and a joint Greek and Turkish military headquarters was also to be established.

THE REPUBLIC OF CYPRUS

The first general election occurred in July 1960. Of the 35 seats allotted to the Greek Cypriots, 30 were won by supporters of Makarios and 5 were allotted to the communist-led Progressive Party of the Working People (AKEL). All 15 Turkish Cypriot seats were won by supporters of Küçük. Cyprus became a republic on August 16, 1960, and was admitted as a member of the UN. The British government agreed to provide financial assistance over a period of five years, and Cyprus gained membership in the Commonwealth in March 1961.

Despite these arrangements, the long-standing conflict between the Greek Cypriot majority and the Turkish Cypriot minority intensified following independence. The difficulties the government encountered in implementing some of the complicated provisions of the constitution, particularly regarding local government and finance, led Makarios to propose 13 amendments to Küçük in late 1963. These were rejected by the Turkish government and the Turkish Cypriots, and fighting broke out between the two Cypriot communities. As a result, the area controlled by the Turkish Cypriots was reduced to a few enclaves, and Nicosia was divided by a cease-fire line—known as the Green Line—policed by British troops. In March 1964 the UN Security Council agreed to send to Cyprus a multinational peacekeeping force, the mandate of which was extended repeatedly as the conflict continued. In 1964 the Turkish air force intervened after intensified fighting broke out in the northwest. Contingents of troops and officers from Greece and Turkey were taken into the island clandestinely to command and train the forces raised by the two communities. Grivas, who had been promoted to lieutenant general in the Greek army, returned from Greece to command the Greek Cypriot National Guard. In 1967 an incident in the southeast led to a Turkish ultimatum to Greece, backed by the threat of invasion. The military junta then ruling Greece complied by withdrawing the mainland contingents and General Grivas. An uneasy peace ensued, but intercommunal talks failed to produce a solution.

Makarios was reelected president in 1968 by an overwhelming majority and won again in 1973. Although he had originally been a leader in the campaign for enosis, many Greek Cypriots and mainland Greeks believed that, by the time he became president, he was content with Cyprus's independence. Angered, dissidents tried to assassinate Makarios in 1970 and 1973, and in 1973 he was denounced by the three suffragan bishops who were ecclesiastically subordinate to him. Meanwhile, Grivas had returned secretly to Cyprus in 1971 to resume the campaign for enosis; he died in Limassol in 1974.

ESTABLISHMENT OF AN INDEPENDENT TURKISH STATE

On July 15, 1974, a detachment of the National Guard, led by officers from mainland Greece, launched a coup to assassinate Makarios and establish enosis. They demolished the presidential palace, but Makarios escaped. A former EOKA member, Nikos Sampson, was proclaimed president of Cyprus. Five days later Turkish forces landed at Kyrenia to overthrow Sampson's government. They were met by vigorous resistance, but the Turks were successful in establishing a

RAUF DENKTASH

Turkish Cypriot politician Rauf Denktash (born January 27, 1924, Paphos, British Cyprus—died January 13, 2012 Nicosia [Lefkosa], North Cyprus) battled throughout his career for a two-state solution to the sectarian division on the island of Cyprus and thus for international recognition of the self-proclaimed (1983) Turkish Republic of Northern Cyprus (TRNC), of which he served as the de facto head of state (under various titles) from February 1973 until he retired in April 2005. Denktash was educated in Nicosia, Cyprus, and Istanbul and pursued legal studies in London before returning to Cyprus to practice law. He then served as a crown prosecutor (1952–56) and acting solicitor general (1956–58), often working for the interests of Turkish Cypriots. He also cofounded the militant Turkish Resistance Organization. After Cyprus obtained independence (1960) from Britain, Denktash was among those who accused the Greek-dominated government of oppressing the Turkish minority and seeking eventual unification with Greece. An abortive military coup within the Greek Cypriot government in 1974 spurred Turkey to send troops to Cyprus, where they seized the northern third of the island and established a Turkish zone led by Denktash. Although only Turkey recognized the TRNC, Denktash steadfastly refused international calls for reunification of the divided island.

bridgehead around Kyrenia and linking it with the Turkish sector of Nicosia. On July 23 Greece's junta fell, and a democratic government under Konstantinos Karamanlis took power. At the same time, Sampson was replaced in Cyprus by Glafcos Clerides, who as president of the House of Representatives automatically succeeded the head of state in the latter's absence. As required by treaty, the three guarantor powers—Britain, Greece, and Turkey—met for discussions in Geneva, but the Turkish advance continued until mid-August. By that time Turkey controlled roughly the northern third of the island. In December Makarios returned and resumed the presidency, and a few months later Turkish leaders proclaimed a Turkish Federated State of Cyprus under Rauf Denktash as president. Since that time the boundary between the two sectors has unofficially been known as "the Attila Line," named for the Turkish army's battle plan.

In May 1983 Denktash broke off all intercommunal talks, and in November he proclaimed the Turkish Republic of Northern Cyprus (TRNC); the republic's independence was recognized only by Turkey. The UN Security Council condemned the move and repeated its demand, first made in 1974, that all foreign troops be withdrawn from the Republic of Cyprus. Renewed UN peace-proposal efforts in 1984 and 1985 were unsuccessful, and in May 1985 a constitution for the TRNC was approved by referendum.

THE FAILURE OF INTERCOMMUNAL TALKS

Negotiations between Clerides and Denktash, representing the Greek and Turkish Cypriots, respectively, had begun in 1968. They continued inconclusively until 1974, the Turks demanding and the Greeks rejecting the proposal for a bizonal federation with a weak central government. In February 1975 the Turkish Cypriots proclaimed the Turkish-occupied area the Turkish Federated State of Cyprus (a body calling itself the Provisional Cyprus-Turkish Administration had been in existence among Turkish Cypriots since 1967); Denktash announced that their purpose was not independence but federation. Talks were resumed in Vienna in 1975 and 1976 under UN auspices, and in early 1977 Makarios and Denktash agreed on acceptable guidelines for a bizonal federation.

In August 1977 Makarios died, and Spyros Kyprianou, president of the House of Representatives, became acting president of the republic; he returned unopposed to that office for a five-year term in January 1978 and was reelected in 1983; Turkish Cypriots took no part in the 1983 election.

Kyprianou lost his bid for a third term in 1988 to an independent candidate, George Vassiliou. He in turn lost by a narrow margin in 1993 to Clerides, a rightist, who was reelected in 1998. At first Clerides showed no willingness to deal with the Turkish Cypriot leader Denktash, but the two eventually met in New York City under UN auspices. The government of the Republic of Cyprus (composed solely of Greek Cypriots) began applying for membership to the European Union (EU) in 1990, though its admittance was repeatedly blocked by Turkey and its supporters.

In late 2002 the EU offered Cyprus membership in its organization on the condition that reunification talks conclude by March 2003 (barring reunification, membership would go to the Greek Cypriot portion of the country only). Just weeks before the March deadline, Tassos Papadopoulos defeated Clerides and assumed the presidency of the Republic of Cyprus, but no agreement was reached. The following month TRNC leaders relaxed restrictions along the Green Line that divided the island, and, for the first time in some 30 years, Cypriots moved with relative freedom throughout the country. In 2004 Turkish Cypriots voted to accept a UN-backed reunification plan, while the Greek Cypriot community—led by Papadopoulos—overwhelmingly rejected the plan; as a result, Greek Cyprus alone was admitted to the EU in May 2004. Although the TRNC remained unrecognized, in the wake of the TRNC's affirmative vote in the 2004 ballot, the EU expressed interest in reducing its isolation through measures such as aid and direct trade. In spite of this commitment, however, such measures were not immediately forthcoming.

In early 2008 Papadopoulos was narrowly defeated in the first round of voting during the country's presidential elections, a move thought to signal declining support by Greek Cypriots for the country's continued division. Dimitris Christofias, leader of Cyprus's communist party and an advocate of renewed unification efforts, was elected to the presidency shortly thereafter. Soon after his election, Christofias reached an agreement with Mehmet Ali Talat, the leader of the TRNC, to open a crossing at Ledra Street in the divided capital of Nicosia. The division of Ledra Street, split since 1964, had for many come to symbolize the broader partition of the island. Unification talks between Talat and Christofias were under way in later months, although efforts appeared to come under threat in April 2010 with the defeat of Talat and the election of Derviş Eroğlu to the TRNC presidency. However, Eroğlu, who had favoured independence for northern Cyprus over unification, insisted that negotiations would continue under his leadership. In legislative elections in May 2011, gains by the opposition Democratic Rally and a record number of abstentions were interpreted by many as a sign of voter dissatisfaction with the progress of reunification talks.

CHAPTER 6

GREECE: THE LAND AND ITS PEOPLE

G reece is the southernmost of the countries of the Balkan Peninsula, and geography has greatly influenced the country's development. Mountains have historically restricted internal communications, but the sea has opened up wider horizons. The total land area of Greece (one-fifth of which is made up of the Greek islands) is comparable in size to England or the U.S. state of Alabama.

Greece has more than 2,000 islands, of which about 170 are inhabited; some of the easternmost Aegean islands lie just a few miles off the Turkish coast. The country's capital is Athens, which expanded rapidly in the second half of the 20th century. Attikí (ancient Greek: Attica), the area around the capital, is now home to about one-third of the country's entire population.

The flag of Greece. Encyclopaedia Britannica, Inc.

A Greek legend has it that God distributed soil through a sieve and used the stones that remained to build Greece. The country's barren landscape has historically caused the people to migrate. The Greeks, like the Jews and the Armenians, traditionally have been a people of diaspora, and several million people of Greek descent live in various parts of the world. Xeniteia, or sojourning in foreign lands, with its strong overtones of nostalgia for the faraway homeland, has been a central element in the historical experience of the Greek people.

Physical map of Greece. Encyclopaedia Britannica, Inc.

Greece is a country that is at once European, Balkan, Mediterranean, and Near Eastern. It lies at the juncture of Europe, Asia, and Africa and is heir to the heritages of Classical Greece, the Byzantine Empire, and nearly four centuries of Ottoman Turkish rule.

Greece is bordered to the east by the Aegean Sea, to the south by the Mediterranean Sea, and to the west by the Ionian Sea. Only to the north and northeast does it have land borders (totaling some 735 miles [1,180 km]), with, from west to east, Albania, the Republic of Macedonia, Bulgaria, and Turkey. The Greek landscape is conspicuous not only for its rugged beauty but also for its complexity and variety. Three elements dominate: the sea, the mountains, and the lowland. The Greek mainland is sharply indented; arms and inlets of the sea penetrate so deeply that only a small, wedge-shaped portion of the interior is more than 50 miles (80 km) from the coast. The rocky headlands and peninsulas extend outward to the sea where there are many island arcs and archipelagoes. The southernmost part of mainland Greece, the Pelopónnisos (ancient Greek: Peloponnese) peninsula, connects to the mainland only by the narrow isthmus at the head of the Gulf of Korinthiakós (Corinth). Greece's mountainous terrain covers some four-fifths of the country, much of which is deeply dissected. A series of mainland mountain chains running northwest-southeast enclose narrow parallel valleys and numerous small basins that once held lakes. With riverine plains and thin, discontinuous strips of coastal plain, these interior valleys and basins constitute the lowland. Although it accounts for only about one-fifth of the country's land area, the lowland has played an important role in the life of the country.

RELIEF

Three characteristics of geology and structure underlie these landscape elements. First, northeastern Greece is occupied by a stable block of ancient (Hercynian) hard rock. Second, younger and weaker rocks, the majority of which are of limestone origin, make up western and southern Greece. These were heavily folded during the Alp-building phase of the Paleogene and Neogene periods (about 65 to 2.6 million years ago), when Earth movements thrust the softer sediments east-northeast against the unyielding Hercynian block and produced a series of roughly parallel tectonic zones that gave rise to the mountain-and-valley relief. Third, both the Hercynian block and the Hellenidic (Alpine) ranges were subsequently raised and fractured by tectonic movements. These dislocations created the sunken basins of the Ionian and Aegean seas as well as the jagged edges so typical of Greece's landscape. Earthquakes are frequent reminders that similar earth movements continue, particularly along the major fault lines.

One result of the region's geologic instability is the widespread presence of marble, which is limestone that has been altered by pressure and heat. Seismic disturbances are sometimes associated with volcanic explosions, especially those involving the island of Thíra (ancient Greek: Thera; also called Santoríni), which was virtually destroyed by a major eruption in the 2nd millennium BCE. The vents of the Kaméni islands in the sea-filled explosion crater of Thíra remain active. The island of Mílos (Melos), which rises to 2,465 feet (751 metres) above sea level, is composed of young volcanic rocks.

Relief and geology provide the basis for describing the Greek landscape in terms of six major regions: central, northeastern, eastern, southern, and western mainland Greece, along with the islands.

Coastal islands and bays along the Aegean Sea, Greece. Josef Muench.

CENTRAL GREECE

The central mountain range, the Píndos (ancient Greek: Pindus) Mountains, forms the core of mainland Greece. Following the general northwest-southeast trend of the mountains of the Balkan Peninsula, the Píndos sweep down from the Albanian and Macedonian frontiers, creating a powerful barrier. The two passes of Métsovon and Mount Timfristós divide the range into three units: a fairly open segment in the north where impervious shales and sandstones have weathered and formed into extensive upland valleys and gently inclining hills; the Píndos proper in the centre, some 20 miles (32 km) wide and predominantly limestone; and an almost uncrossable zone in the south, about 50 miles (80 km) wide, deeply cut by winding rivers and composed of a mixture of limestone, slates, and sandstones. The range's highest point, Mount Smólikas, 8,652 feet (2,637 metres) high, is found in the north.

NORTHEASTERN GREECE

Several topographic regions surround the main mountainous core and are often penetrated by extensions of it. The northernmost part, roughly the regions of Greek Makedonía (Macedonia) and Thráki (Thrace), extends in a long, narrow, east-west band between the Aegean coast and the frontier with the countries of Macedonia and Bulgaria. It consists of forest-clad, crystalline mountain massifs and plateaus created by the fracturing of the Hercynian block and separated from each other by the alluvial deposits of the five great rivers of northern Greece:

the Maritsa (Évros), Néstos, Strymónas (Struma), Vardaráis (Vardar; Axiós;), and Aliákmonos (Aliákmon). The fracturing of the Hercynian also accounts for the odd three-pronged shape of the Chalkidikí (Chalcidice) Peninsula, on whose easternmost prong is located Mount Athos (Holy Mountain), the famous site of Greek Orthodox monastic communities. Along and beyond the Bulgarian border rise the Rodópi (Rhodope) Mountains, mainly composed of sharp-edged and sloping plateaus, reaching 7,260 feet (2,213 metres) at Mount Órvilos. The Maritsa River, in its low-lying, marshy valley, marks the Turkish border. From there to the lower Strymónas River extends a succession of plains, some of which are often swampy, such as the deltaic plain of the lower Néstos, and others have been turned into fertile agricultural land, as is the case in the former Lake Akhinós. Inland there are basins of structural origin, such as the Drámas (Drama) Plain. Lakes Koróneia (Korónia) and Vólvi, which separate the Chalkidikí Peninsula from the rest of the coastal region, also occupy structural depressions. Farther west, the large plain drained by the Vardaráis and lower Aliákmonos rivers is being continually extended as the river deltas push out into the Gulf of Thermaïkós (Thérmai). The forested Vérmion (Vérmio) Mountains and, beyond them, the barren inland basins around Lakes Vegorítida (Vegorrítis) and Kardítsa mark the boundary with the Píndos Mountains.

EASTERN GREECE

The western part of this region contains the massive limestone formations so characteristic of northern and western Greece, while to the east the peninsula of Attiikí (Attica) represents the western margin of the Hercynian crystalline rocks of the Aegean shores. Essentially an upland area, its relief is articulated by four northwest–southeast-trending spurs thrusting out from the main Píndos mass. A number of distinctive basins and plains lie amid these upland ribs. The northernmost, a rather broken spur called the Kamvoúnia Mountains, runs along the coast of the Gulf of Thermaïkós and continues south to form the peninsula bounding one side of Vólou Bay. Among its peaks are Mount Ólympos (Olympus)—the mythical seat of the gods, whose often cloud-topped summit rises to 9,570 feet (2,917 metres), the highest point in Greece—and the equally fine peaks of Mounts Kisszavos (Ossa) and Pílios (Pelion). The next spur to the west is the Óthris mountain range, which continues across the narrow Oreón Channel in the northern sector of the long, narrow island of Évvoia (Euboea). Between the two spurs lie the ancient basins (formerly the site of lakes) of Thessalía (Thessaly), Tríkala, and Lárisa, drained by the Pineiós (Piniós) River. Just to the south the basin of Almyrós (Almirós), of similar origin, lies around Vólou Bay.

To the southwest the third spur leaving the Píndos is that of the Oíti, which continues in the Óchi (Ókhi) Mountains of southern Évvoia. Just before the Oíti reaches the sea, near the head of the Gulf of Maliakós, is the pass of Thermopýles (Thermopylae, scene of the famous battle of antiquity). The last (and perhaps the most important) of the four spurs thrusting down into eastern Greece is the one that curves away to the southeast through the twin-peaked mass of Mount Parnassós (Parnassus). This mountain, rising to an elevation of 8,061 feet (2,457 metres), was held to be the home of the Muses. The view from its summit at sunrise, with a broad expanse of the heart of Greece gradually unfolding, is regarded as one of the finest in the world. The range continues as the backbone of the peninsula lying between the Gulf of Évvoia and the Gulf of Korinthiakós (Corinth), and it reaches as far as Mount Párnis, just to the north of Athens. To its north lie the plains of Fokída (Phocis) and Voiotía (Boeotia), and around its southern tip lie the hotter and more arid depressions of Attiikí.

SOUTHERN GREECE

The entire southern portion of mainland Greece forms a peninsula lying to the south of the Gulf of Korinthiakós. Technically, this region, the Pelopónnisos, also known as the Morea, is now an island, for the 3.9-mile (6.3-km) Korinthiakós Canal cuts across the narrow neck of land that formerly separated the Gulf of Korinthiakós from that of Aígina (Aíyina). The Pelopónnisos consists of an oval-shaped mountain mass with peaks rising

to 7,800 feet (2,400 metres) and four peninsular prongs, which point southward toward the island of Crete (Modern Greek: Kríti). At its heart are the arid limestone plateaus of Arkadía (Arcadia), where streams disappear underground into the soluble rock and from which the barren upland of the Táygetos (Taïyetos) Mountains, reaching an elevation of 7,800 feet, extends southward to form the backbone of one of the southern peninsulas. A thin fringe of fertile coastal plain in the north and west, together with the larger alluvial depressions forming the Gulfs of Lakonia (Laconia), Messenía (Kalamata), and Argolikós (Árgolis), surrounds this mountainous core. The coast is indented and has some harbours.

WESTERN GREECE

Western Greece consists of Ípeiros (Epirus) and Arkánanion, which is the area north of the Gulf of Korinthiakós to the Albanian frontier, and is often considered to include the offshore Iónia (Ionian) Islands. The distinctiveness of western Greece is enhanced by the fact that the barrier effect of the Píndos and the ameliorating climatic influences from the west result in a quite different landscape from that of the rest of Greece. The west's physical attributes have exaggerated its historical isolation from the other areas of mainland Greece. Fertile basins are not well developed, constricted as they are by the parallel ranges of the coastal mountains. The mountain regions themselves, however,

The church of St. Sophia at the ruined Byzantine city of Mistra, Greece, on a spur of the Táygetos (Taïyetos) Mountains overlooking olive groves in the Evrótas River valley, in the Pelopónnisos (Peloponnese). David Warren/Superstock.

are adequately supplied with precipitation. The flat, alluvial plain of Árta, built up from detritus brought down by the Árachthos (Árakhthos) River has become, with irrigation, a fertile agricultural region.

THE ISLANDS OF GREECE

The Ionian Islands off the western coast of Greece structurally resemble the folded mountains of Ípeiros. Of the six main islands, Corfu (Modern Greek: Kérkyra), opposite the Albanian frontier, is the northernmost; it is fertile and amply endowed with well-watered lowland. The other islands, Paxoí (Paxos), Lefkáda (Leucas), Itháki (Ithaca), Kefaloniá (Cephallenia), and Zákynthos (Zacynthus), lie farther south; lack of rainfall accentuates their gaunt, broken limestone relief, although Lefkáda and Zákynthos have sheltered eastern plains. A seventh island, Kýthira (Cythera), is grouped with the Ionian Islands for administrative purposes but is geographically discrete. The Aegean islands, also exhibiting the characteristic landforms of the mainland, are situated in distinct clusters in the Aegean Sea, east of the Greek mainland.

In the north, off Thráki (Thrace), lie Thásos, an oval block of ancient mineral rocks similar in composition to neighbouring blocks on the mainland, and harbourless Samothráki (Samothrace), an island of volcanic origin. Límnos (Lemnos), situated midway between Asia Minor and the Mount Athós peninsula, is almost cut in two by the northern Pourniás Bay and the deep southern harbour afforded by the Bay of Moúdros (Moúdhrou).

To the southeast the rocky but sheltered islands of Lésbos (Lésvos), Chíos (Khíos), and Sámos lie close to the Turkish

The harbour and town of Mytilene, view from the citadel, Lésbos, Greece. Tomas Friedmann/Photo Researchers

coast and are extensions of peninsulas on the coast of Asia Minor. Across the central Aegean, near northern Évvoia, lie the Northern Sporades ("Scattered Islands"); their crystalline rocks are similar to those of the Greek mainland. Farther south, in the heart of the Aegean, lie the Kykládes (Cyclades; "Islands in a Circle"). These roughly centre on Dílos (Delos) and represent the tips of drowned mountain ridges continuing the structural trends of Évvoia and the region around Athens.

Between the Kykládes and the Turkish coast, Dodekánisa (the Dodecanese group), of which Ródos (Rhodes) is the largest of a dozen major islands, has a varied geologic structure ranging from the gray limestones of Kálymnos (Kálimnos), Sými (Sími), and Chálki to the complete ancient volcanic cone that forms Nísuros (Nísiros).

A 17th-century bridge over the Árachthos River, Árta, Greece. Babette and Marshall Druck /Photo Researchers

Finally, the long narrow shape of Crete stands to the south at the entrance of the Aegean. With an area of 3,190 square miles (8,262 square km), it is by far the largest of the Aegean islands and the fifth largest island in the Mediterranean. Crete is geologically linked to the south and west of mainland Greece. Its rugged, deeply ravined, asymmetrical limestone massif, falling steeply to the south, from a distance resembles four separate islands: the westernmost Lefká (Levká) Mountains; the central Psíloreítis (Ídi) Mountains, with Crete's highest point, the summit of Mount Psíloreítis, called Timios Stavrós, 8,058 feet (2,456 metres) high; the east-central Díkti Mountains; and the far eastern Tryptí (Thriptís) Mountains. Another range, the Asteroúsia (Kófinas) Mountains, runs along the south-central coast between the Mesarás Plain and the Libyan Sea. Of Crete's 650

miles (1,050 km) of rocky coastline, it is the more gradual slope on the northern side of the island that provides several natural harbours and coastal plains.

DRAINAGE

The main rivers of Greece share several characteristics. In their upper courses, most flow in broad, gently sloping valleys, while in their middle courses, they plunge through a series of intermontane basins in narrow, often spectacular gorges. Finally, in their lower courses, they meander across the coastal plain to reach the sea in marshy, ever-growing deltas.

Most of the country's rivers are short. In limestone districts a generally permeable surface with sinkholes (*katavóthra*) leading to underground channels complicates the drainage network. River regimes in all regions are erratic, unsuitable for navigation, and of limited usefulness for irrigation.

The Vardaráis, Strymónas, and Néstos, which cross Greek Makedonía and Thráki to enter the northern Aegean, are the major rivers, but only because they drain large regions beyond the Greek frontier. Also in the northeast are the eastward-flowing Aliákmonos and Piniós, and in the Pelopónnisos is the Evrótas, which flows southeastward into the Gulf of Lakonia.

SOILS

Throughout the rocky highland areas of Greece, which are characterized by their limestone formations, the soil is thin and relatively poor. The valley areas contain claylike soil known as terra rosa, reddened earth that originates from the residue of limestone rocks. These areas are adequate for farming. The most fertile regions, however, are along coastal plains and beside rivers. The clay and loam soils that predominate there may even require drainage prior to cultivation.

CLIMATE

The Mediterranean climate of Greece is subject to a number of regional and local variations based on the country's physical diversity. In winter the belt of low-pressure disturbances moving in from the North Atlantic Ocean shifts southward, bringing with it warm, moist, westerly winds. As the low-pressure areas enter the Aegean region, they may draw in cold air from those eastern regions of the Balkans that, sheltered by the Dinaric mountain system from western influences, are open to climatic extremes emanating from the heart of Eurasia. This icy wind is known as the boreas. Partly as a result, Thessaloníki (Salonika; Thessalonica) has an average January temperature in the low 40s F (about 6 °C), while in Athens it is in the low 50s F (about 10 °C), and in Iráklieo (Candia) on Crete it is in the low to mid-50s F (about 12 °C). Occasionally the warmer sirocco (*shilok*) winds are drawn in from the south. The western climatic influences bring plenty of precipitation to the Ionian coast and the mountains behind it;

winter rain starts early, and snow lingers into spring. On Corfu, January temperatures average in the low 50s F (10 °C), and the island's average annual precipitation is about 52 inches (1,320 mm), compared with that on Crete of about 25 inches (640 mm) and that at Athens of about 16 inches (400 mm). Few populated areas have lasting snowfalls, but snow is commonly found on the highest peaks.

In summer, when the low-pressure belt swings away again, the climate is hot and dry almost everywhere. The average July sea-level temperature approaches 80 °F (27 °C), although heat waves can push the temperature well above 100 °F (38 °C) for a day or so. Topography is again a modifying factor: the interior northern mountains continue to experience some precipitation, while along the winding coast the afternoon heat is eased slightly by sea breezes. In other regions, such as Crete, the hot, dry summers are accentuated by the parching meltemi, or etesian winds, which become drier as they are drawn southward.

In all seasons—perhaps especially in summer—the quality of light is one of Greece's most appealing attractions. However, atmospheric pollution has become a serious problem in the cities, notably Athens, obscuring the sky and posing a hazard to the ancient monuments.

PLANT AND ANIMAL LIFE

As in other Balkan countries, the vegetation of Greece is open to influences from

Maquis (macchie) vegetation on the Mediterranean coast, near Sithonía, Greece. Oleg Polunin

several major biogeographic zones, with the major Mediterranean and western Asian elements supplemented by plants and animals from the central European interior. The subtle but complex vegetation mosaic is a product of the climatic effects of elevation, the contrast between north and south, local relief, and eight or nine millennia of human settlement and land use. Degraded plant associations (areas where the variety and size of species and the density of plant cover are reduced) and soil erosion are common.

Vegetation types from central Europe prevail on the mountain flanks and generally in the north. In central and

southern regions and in the narrow belts along the valleys of the mountains, about half the land is under scrub of various kinds; and maquis—the classic Mediterranean scrub, with oleander, bay, evergreen oak, olive, and juniper—is especially prevalent in the Pelopónnisos. Evergreen trees and shrubs and herbaceous plants are found in the lowland, their flowers offering brilliant patterns in springtime. Pines, plane trees, and poplars line the rivers, the higher slopes, and the coastal plains. Forests and scrub are found at the highest elevations; black pine forests cover Mount Ólympos. Oak, chestnut, and other deciduous trees are found in the north, giving way at higher elevations to coniferous forests dominated by the Grecian fir, in which clearings are carpeted in spring and summer with irises, crocuses, and tulips. Greece is home to about 6,000 species of wildflowers, of which some 600 are endemic.

The forested zones, especially in the north, harbour such European mammals as wildcats, martens, brown bears, roe deer, and, more rarely, wolves, wild boars, and lynx. Animals of the Mediterranean regions include hares, wild goats, and porcupines, all adapted to the heat and lack of moisture. Birds include owls, vultures, pelicans, storks, and herons, and many varieties from farther north spend the winter in Greece, while others stop on Greek land and water while migrating to and from Africa. Reptile and marine life have come under increasing pressure, the former by overdevelopment and the latter by exhaustive fishing.

ETHNIC GROUPS

The population of Greece, in particular that of northern Greece, has always been characterized by a great deal of ethnic, religious, and linguistic diversity. Migrations, invasions, imperial conquests, and 20th-century wars all contributed to this cultural diversity, which continues to characterize modern Greece, in spite of several instances of population exchanges that occurred as a result of treaties between Greece and Bulgaria in 1919 and between Greece and Turkey in 1923, along with long-standing government policies of assimilation, or Hellenization. According to the dominant ideology of the Greek state, all the people of Greece are, or should be, Greek. As a result, the existence of ethnic and national diversity in the country has remained a sensitive issue. The Greek government's official position is that there are no ethnic or national minorities in the country and that virtually the entire population is Greek. The only minority officially recognized by the Greek government is a religious minority, the Muslim minority of Thráki (Thrace), whose existence was acknowledged in the 1923 Treaty of Lausanne. Nonetheless, the population of Greece includes people who identify themselves as Turks, Macedonians, Albanians, Aromani (Vlachs), and Roma (Gypsies). With the exception of Cyprus, southern Albania, and Turkey, there are no major enclaves of Greeks in nearby countries, although Greek expatriate communities play a distinctive role in Europe, North and South America, Australia, and South Africa.

LANGUAGES

The Greek language is one of the oldest Indo-European languages, its antecedents dating to about the 17th century BCE. Koine (the language of the New Testament) and Byzantine Greek represent the middle phases of Greek. These ultimately gave way in the 19th century CE to Modern Greek (except in the liturgy of the Greek Orthodox Church, which still uses Koine). Modern Greek comprises Standard Modern Greek and the various regional dialects. Standard Modern Greek is the official state language, and it is an amalgamation of two historical forms: Demotic, which is widely spoken, and Katharevusa, an archaistic form that was primarily written, appearing in official government documents and newspapers until the mid-1970s. Separate transliteration tables are generally used for Classical and Modern Greek; however, changes in the pronunciation of the Greek language and conflicting transliteration conventions have resulted in widespread discrepancies even in the rendering of

KATHAREVUSA AND DEMOTIC GREEK

The emergence of a Greek national identity in the 19th century and the development of a modern, independent Greek state were accompanied by the development of two distinct varieties of the Greek language: Katharevusa, an artificial, purist form of modern Greek, and Demotic, a vernacular form.

Although the vocabulary, phonology, and grammar of ancient Greek remained the basis of spoken Greek in the postclassical and modern eras, by the beginning of the 19th century the language had been considerably modified and simplified. Foreign words and constructions had been introduced in large numbers, reflecting the influences of various foreign powers that held sway over Greece or that exerted influence there, from the foundation of the eastern Roman Empire (325 CE) through the Crusades to the Venetian and Turkish conquests. The Turkish domination, in particular, destroyed Greek literary continuity and development, and after Greece regained its independence in the early 19th century, many nationalists—wishing to meet the need for a uniform written language—developed an artificial, purified language, Katharevusa, as an approximation of the old classical norms. It was a deliberate archaization meant to purge the language of foreign elements and to systematize its morphology by using ancient Greek roots and much classical inflection. Its syntax differed only slightly from that of Demotic, the spoken language, but it was much more resistant to loanwords. Following Greek independence, Katharevusa flourished in the Romantic literary school of Athens; it is exemplified in the classical odes, hymns, ballads, narrative poems, tragedies, and comedies of Aléxandros Rízos Rangavís and in the verses of Akhilléfs Paráskhos, characterized by rhetorical profuseness and mock-heroic patriotism. Katharevusa was also institutionalized as the language of education, administration, and the press.

The turn toward Demotic began in the late 1800s, led by poets and writers who rejected Katharevusa as stilted and artificial. Tensions between proponents of Demotic and Katharevusa began to take on political overtones, and even led to rioting in Athens in 1901. Over the first half of the 20th century, successive governments introduced a variety of measures expanding recognition of Demotic alongside Katharevusa.

When a military dictatorship arose in 1967, the new conservatism extended to language, and Katharevusa was strictly imposed in the schools. But after the restoration of political democracy in 1974, linguistic democracy followed suit, and Demotic—literally, the "popular" language—was given official sanction. Many Katharevusa elements were incorporated into Demotic, and today the two varieties have merged to form Standard Modern Greek (known in Greek as Koini Neoelliniki).

Modern Greek names in Roman orthography. Although not officially recognized, minority languages spoken in the country include Turkish, Macedonian, Albanian, Aromanian (the dialect of Romanian spoken by the Aromani [Vlachs]; also called Macedo-Romanian), Bulgarian, and Romany.

RELIGION

Despite the long Ottoman administration, virtually all of the population belongs to the Church of Greece (Greek Orthodox Church). This body appoints its own ecclesiastical hierarchy and is headed by a synod of 12 metropolitans under the presidency of the archbishop of Athens. The Greek church shares some doctrines with the other Eastern Orthodox churches. Virtually all Cretans belong to a special branch of the Church of Greece, headed by the archbishop of Crete, who is directly responsible to the Ecumenical Patriarchate of Constantinople, as are the monks of Mount Athos.

The Muslim (primarily Sunni) minority, which constitutes most of the non-Orthodox sector of the population, is mainly Turkish and concentrated in western Thráki and the Dodecanese. Roman and Greek Catholics, predominantly located in Athens and the western islands formerly under Italian rule, account for the rest, except for a few thousand adherents of Protestantism and Judaism. Greece's Jewish population was almost wiped out by the Nazi genocide of World War II.

CHURCH OF GREECE

The Church of Greece is Greece's established church and one of the most important autocephalous, or ecclesiastically independent, churches of the Eastern Orthodox communion.

During the Byzantine Empire and the subsequent Turkish occupation of Greece, the Christian church in Greece was under the administration of the ecumenical patriarch of Constantinople. After the Greek War of Independence (1821–32), Ioánnis Kapodístrias, the provisional president of Greece, opened negotiations with the patriarch for the independence of the Greek church. The final decision was taken during the minority of the new king of Greece, Otto I, through his Protestant regent, G.L. Maurer, who, fearing that the Turkish government might still be able to influence Greek politics through the ecumenical patriarchate, declared the Greek church autocephalous in 1833. Its independence was recognized by the ecumenical patriarch in 1850.

The Church of Greece is organized as a state church according to the pattern adopted in Russia under Peter the Great. Supreme authority is vested in the synod of all the bishops under the presidency of the archbishop of Athens and all Greece. A second synod, under the same presidency, consists of 12 bishops, each serving for one year only. The former deals with general church questions, the latter with details of administration. With more than 10 million faithful at the beginning of the 21st century, the church is divided into 81 small dioceses; 20 of these, in northern Greece and in the islands, are nominally under the jurisdiction of Constantinople. Only a small minority of the church's priests have a university education. Many village and town priests have little formal training beyond two years at higher seminaries after high school. The theological faculties at the universities of Athens and Thessaloníki train candidates for the

episcopate, as well as religious teachers who remain laymen.

Orthodoxy as a popular religion still retains a powerful hold on the country, and the Church of Greece's adaptation to the modern secularized world has proved a major problem. Several monastic communities, chiefly the monastic republic of Mount Athos, are the main strongholds of the traditional forms. Although not approaching the numbers it once boasted, monasticism—especially at the monastery of Longovorda and the monastery of Saint John the Evangelist on Pátmos and on Mount Athos —enjoyed a resurgence in the late 20th and early 21st centuries.

Greek Orthodox priests from the monastery of St. John the Theologian celebrating an outdoor Easter service on Pátmos (Patmos), a Greek island of the Dodekánisa (Dodecanese) group in the Aegean Sea. © John Sims—CLICK/ Chicago

SETTLEMENT PATTERNS

In terms of human geography, Greece can be described as "classical Mediterranean" and "Balkan." History rather than the physical environment accounts for the variations in settlement patterns, social composition, and demographic trends that cannot be explained by differentiating between "Old Greece" and the territories annexed in the early 20th century. For example, although

Greece is considered an "old country," relatively densely populated in prehistoric times and well settled and much exploited in and since ancient times (as the large number of Classical monuments and important archaeological sites testifies), instability is as characteristic of Greece's settlement pattern as it is of its history. New villages, associated not only with Ottoman colonization but also with agrarian reform in the first three decades of the 20th century, are neighbours to some of the most ancient towns of Mediterranean Europe, notably Khaniá (Chaniá), Pýlos, Thíra (Santoríni), Árgos, Athens, Spárti (Sparta), and Thíva (Thebes). Traditionally, towns and villages have depended on the fertility of the surrounding land. Isolation, which contributes to this self-sufficiency (the autarkeia of the ancient city-states), survives in the remote villages of mountainous Greece. Only Corinth (Modern Greek: Kórinthos) and Athens were major trading centres in ancient times. The other trading areas were located where sea and land routes coincided with cultivatable land. From the Byzantine period onward, fortification became an essential factor for both monastic and secular settlement, emphasizing the importance of the mountain regions and of "perched" sites above lowland. As late as the 1960s, about two-fifths of Greece's population lived in mountain regions. A return to the plains took place during intermittent periods of relative stability, and the settlement pattern, dispersed or nucleated and often geometrically laid out, thus always seems to be "new."

Greeks have preserved a strong sense of community, and village life remains a powerful influence. This holds true despite the decline of the rural population, which now constitutes about two-fifths of Greece's total population. The same may be said about the small villages and towns at the bottom of the urban hierarchy. At the other end of the urban scale, however, Greece's larger

Street on the island of Mýkonos (Míkonos), Greece. Myron Goldfinger, New York

towns and cities have gained considerably in size and commercial importance since the 1970s. The Athens metropolitan area is by far the largest urban concentration, but towns such as Thessaloníki, Pátrai, Vólos, Lárissa (Lárisa), and Iráklion (on Crete) are all fast-growing centres. Of the three-fifths of the population that is urban, a relatively small slice is classified as semiurban. Urbanization

ATHENS

Athens, the capital, is located inland near its port, Piraeus, on the Saronic Gulf in eastern Greece. The source of many of the West's intellectual and artistic conceptions, including that of democracy, Athens is generally considered the birthplace of Western civilization. An ancient city-state, it had by the 6th century BCE begun to assert its influence. It was destroyed by Xerxes in 480 BCE, but rebuilding began immediately. By 450 BCE, led by Pericles, it was at the height of its commercial prosperity and cultural and political dominance, and over the next 40 years many major building projects, including the Acropolis and Parthenon, were completed. Athens's "Golden Age" saw the works of the philosophers Socrates, Plato, and Aristotle; the dramatists Sophocles, Aristophanes, and Euripides; the historians Herodotus, Thucydides, and Xenophon; and the sculptors Praxiteles and Phidias. The Peloponnesian Wars with Sparta ended in Athens's defeat in 404, but it quickly recovered its independence and prosperity. After 338 BCE Athens came under Macedonia's hegemony, which was lifted with the aid of Rome in 197 BCE in a battle at Cynoscephalae. It became subject to Rome in 146 BCE. In the 13th century Athens was taken by the Crusaders. It was conquered in 1456 by the Ottoman Turks, who held it until 1833, when it was declared the capital of independent Greece. Athens is Greece's principal centre for business and foreign trade. The city's ruins and many museums make it a major tourist destination. It hosted the 2004 Olympic Games.

is extending into the countryside, where agrarian reform has severely fragmented landholdings and attracted urban-based financial and marketing entrepreneurs.

DEMOGRAPHIC TRENDS

Most of the country's growth in the years after Greece gained its independence from the Ottomans in 1832 resulted from two factors: annexations of surrounding areas—the Ionian Islands (1864), Thessalía and Árta (1881); Ípeiros, Greek Makedonía, and Crete (1913); Thráki (1920); and the Dodecanese (1947)—and the influx of some 1.5 million Greek refugees from Asia Minor in the 1920s as a result of the Treaty of Lausanne. Emigration was significant in 1911–15, and it became particularly heavy after World War II. The most common destinations of the emigrants were the United States, Canada, Australia, and, somewhat later, Germany, Belgium, and Italy.

The 1950s and '60s were demographically stagnant, but in the 1970s population growth was revitalized. This was, however, almost wholly because of international population movements rather than from an increase in natural growth rates, which remained low. At the middle of the first decade of the new millennium the majority of immigrants were from central and eastern Europe, primarily Albania, followed by Bulgaria, Romania, and Ukraine. Within Greece the contrast between regions losing population (two-thirds of the southern Pelopónnisos; all the Ionian Islands except Corfu; the mountains of central, southwestern, and northeastern mainland Greece; and most of the islands of the eastern Aegean) and those rapidly gaining people (Attikí and other districts outside the major cities) held social and political implications. In the early 21st century, as the fertility rate remained below the replacement rate and as immigration slowed, the overall population growth rate declined. Although the life expectancy of Greek men and women was for some time slightly longer than that in other western European countries, this difference has been decreasing since the late 20th century because of changes in the diet and activities of Greeks.

CHAPTER 7

THE GREEK ECONOMY

Greece's economy underwent rapid growth in the post-World War II period, but it has remained one of the least developed in the European Union (EU). The country's natural resources are limited, its industrialization process has been slow, and it has struggled with the balance of payments. Shipping, tourism, and remittances from expatriate workers (the last of which have been decreasing steadily) are the mainstays of the economy.

Although the Greek economy traditionally has been based on free enterprise, many sectors of the economy have come under direct or, through the banks, indirect government control. This process of establishing state ownership of the economy has been associated with both right and centre-left governments; however, in the first decade of the 21st century, the centre-right government—partly in response to pressure from the EU—showed an inclination for privatizing some sectors. Trade unions, which are fragmented and highly politicized, wield significant power only in the public sector. Measures taken since the late 1980s, however, have begun to decrease the degree of state control of economic activity. Following entry into the European Economic Community (later succeeded by the EU), Greece became a major beneficiary of the Common Agricultural Policy, which provided subsidies to the country's generally inefficient agricultural sector and for projects to improve its infrastructure. Rates of productivity, however, have remained low for both agriculture and industry, and the development of the country's economy has lagged behind that of its EU partners. Unemployment, which historically has been low, grew in the last decades of the 20th century as temporary migrant workers returned to Greece and as demand for immigrant labour has declined in other European countries.

In late 2009 the Greek economy went into a tailspin. This economic and financial crisis had been partly precipitated by the global financial downturn that soured economies throughout the world in 2008–09 in the wake of the burst of the "housing bubble" in the United States in 2007, which left banks around the world awash in "toxic" debt. Beyond the difficulties tied to the international situation, however, it became clear that Greece had its own acute problems derived largely from excessive government borrowing and misleading accounting that had hidden the extent of the government's extraordinary debt. Severe austerity measures were not enough to rescue the Greek economy and government, and in March and April of 2010 the EU and the International Monetary Fund (IMF) —fearing the collapse of the euro currency zone, which Greece had joined in 2001—stepped in with two huge aid packages that came loaded with new demands for austerity measures.

AGRICULTURE, FORESTRY, AND FISHING

Greece's agricultural potential is hampered by poor soil, inadequate levels of

Olive and cypress trees against the mountainous background of northern Corfu (Kérkyra), Greece. Ion Gardey—Robert Harding Picture Library, London

precipitation, a landholding system that has served to increase the number of unproductive smallholdings, and population migration from thew countryside to cities and towns. Less than one-third of the land area is cultivable, with the remainder consisting of pasture, scrub, and forest. Only in the plains of Thessalía, Makedonía, and Thráki is cultivation possible on a reasonably large scale. There corn (maize), wheat, barley, sugar beets, peaches, tomatoes, cotton (of which Greece is the only EU producer), and tobacco are grown.

Other crops grown in considerable quantities are olives (for olive oil), grapes, melons, potatoes, and oranges, all of which are exported to other EU countries. Since the last quarter of the 20th century, Greece also has been exporting hothouse-grown vegetables to northern Europe during the winter. Greek wine, including the resin-flavoured retsina, has been produced primarily for domestic consumption, but by the 1990s Greece was producing wines of higher quality for the world market. Sheep, goats, pigs, cattle, and chickens are raised for export and local consumption.

Although inefficient, Greek agriculture has benefited substantially from EU subsidies, and there are many signs of growing rural prosperity. In general, however, the importance of the agricultural sector to the economy is diminishing.

Forests, mostly state-owned, cover approximately one-fifth of the land area, but they are prone to major forest fires. Forest products make no significant contribution to the economy.

Greece's extensive coastline and numerous islands have always supported intensive fishing activity. However, overfishing and the failure to conserve fish stocks properly, a problem throughout the Mediterranean, have reduced the contribution of fishing to the economy.

RESOURCES AND POWER

Greece has few natural resources. Its only substantial mineral deposits are of nonferrous metals, notably bauxite. The country also has small deposits of silver ore and marble, which are mined. Fossil fuels, with the exception of lignite, are in short supply: there are no deposits of bituminous coal, and oil production, based on the Prinos field near the island of Thásos, is limited. After the Thásos discovery, a dispute developed in the 1970s between Greece and Turkey over the delineation of the two countries' respective continental shelves and has remained unresolved. At the start of the 21st century, about nine-tenths of Greece's electrical power needs were supplied by fossil fuels (primarily by lignite-fueled power stations), and nearly one-tenth by hydroelectric power, with a still considerably smaller slice provided by nuclear energy. From the late 1990s the country began developing solar and wind power.

MANUFACTURING

The manufacturing sector in Greece is weak. An established tradition exists only for the production of textiles, processed foods, and cement. One of the world's largest cement factories is located in Vólos. In the past, private investment was oriented much more toward real estate than toward industry, and concrete apartment blocks proliferated throughout the country. In the 1960s and '70s Greek shipowners took advantage of an investment regime that benefited from foreign capital by investing in such sectors as oil refining and shipbuilding. Shipping continues to be a key industrial sector—the merchant fleet being one of the largest in the world—though many of Greece's ships are older than those of other leading countries. In the 1970s many ships that had hitherto registered under flags of convenience returned to the Greek flag; only a small proportion remains under foreign registry. Greek ships, which are predominantly bulk carriers, are extremely vulnerable to downturns in international economic activity, as they are principally engaged in carrying cargoes between developing countries. In the early 21st century less than one-fifth of the labour force was employed in manufacturing and construction.

FINANCE

The central bank is the Bank of Greece, which issued the drachma, the national currency, until 2001, when Greece adopted the euro as its sole currency. Greece has been a member of the EU since 1981. A significant number of the country's commercial banks are state-controlled. The state also exercises considerable control over the insurance sector.

There is a stock exchange in Athens, but, for many Greeks, real estate, foreign currency, gold, and jewelry have proved to be more attractive investments than securities and bonds. Although Greece has a pension

DRACHMA

The drachma is a silver coin of ancient Greece, dating from about the mid-6th century BCE, and the former monetary unit of modern Greece. The drachma was one of the world's earliest coins. Its name derives from the Greek verb meaning "to grasp," and its original value was equivalent to that of a handful of arrows. The early drachma had different weights in different regions. From the 5th century BCE, Athens gained commercial preeminence, and the Athenian drachma became the foremost currency. One drachma equaled 6 oboli; 100 drachmas equaled 1 mine; and 60 mine equaled 1 Attic talent.

As a result of the conquests of Alexander the Great, the Athenian drachma came to be the monetary unit of the Hellenistic world. In time, silver coins of one drachma and its multiples were debased, and progressively higher proportions of copper were admixed. The drachma also became the prototype of an Islamic coin—the dirham. Nevertheless, as foreign invaders gained control in Greece, the drachma disappeared from use.

When Greece finally achieved its independence from the Ottoman Empire in 1828, the phoenix was introduced as the monetary unit; its use was short-lived, however, and in 1832 the phoenix was replaced by the drachma, adorned with the image of King Otto, who reigned as modern Greece's first king from 1832 to 1862. The drachma was divided into 100 lepta. In 2002 the drachma ceased to be legal tender after the euro, the monetary unit of the European Union, became Greece's sole currency.

and social insurance system of considerable complexity, many Greeks have opposed changes to it. By the late 1990s it had become easier for Greeks to obtain their pensions and get medical care. The main social security fund, the Social Insurance Institute (IKA), is prone to recurrent funding crises.

TRADE

At the beginning of the 21st century, about two-fifths of Greece's trade was with the other member countries of the EU, and its main trading partners were Germany and Italy. The principal exports included food (especially fruit and nuts), clothing and apparel, machinery, and refined petroleum and petroleum-based products. Machinery and transportation equipment, chemicals and chemical products, foodstuffs, ships and boats, and crude petroleum are the country's main imports.

The emergence of a consumer society created a huge demand for imported consumer goods—in particular, automobiles—which had negative consequences for the country's balance of trade. In the early 21st century, the deficit in the balance of payments was offset by the borrowing that would eventually be responsible for the country's economic collapse, as well as by limited foreign investment, and, to a lesser extent, by remittances from emigrants.

The new market (left) above the port of Mandrákion in the city of Ródos (Rhodes), Greece. Gerald Clyde—FPG

SERVICES

Services have become the dominant sector of Greece's economy, contributing about two-thirds of the gross domestic product (GDP) and employing about the same proportion of the workforce by the early 2000s. Government services were significantly reduced, however, as part of the austerity measures undertaken in response to the economic crisis at the end of the decade.

A host of World Heritage sites are found in Greece, including the Acropolis in Athens (designated a World Heritage site in 1987), the medieval city of Rhodes (1988), and the archaeological site of Olympia (1989), to name but a few. Starting in the 1960s, the number of tourists, notably those from European countries, increased significantly, although Greece

ACROPOLIS

An acropolis (Greek: "city at the top") is a central, defensively oriented district in ancient Greek cities, located on the highest ground and containing the chief municipal and religious buildings. Because the founding of a city was a religious act, the establishment of a local home for the gods was a basic factor in Greek city planning. From both a religious and a military point of view, a hilltop site was highly desirable: militarily, because an acropolis had to be a citadel; religiously, because a hill was imbued with natural mysteries—caves, springs, copses, and glens—that denoted the presence of the gods.

Athens has the best-known acropolis, built during the second half of the 5th century BCE. The Athenian acropolis, located on a craggy, walled hill, was built as a home of Athena, the patron goddess of the city. The structures that survive consist of the Propylaea, the gateway to the sacred precinct; the Parthenon, the chief shrine to Athena and also the treasury of the Delian League; the Erechtheum, a shrine to the agricultural deities, especially Erichthonius; and the Temple of Athena Nike, an architectural symbol of the harmony with which the Dorian and Ionian peoples lived under the government of Athens.

faced increasing competition from countries such as Portugal and Turkey. Improved road transport and infrastructure and the creation of a network of truck- and car-carrying ferries linking mainland Greece to the numerous islands and to Italy were instrumental to this growth. By the beginning of the 21st century, some 14 million visitors were arriving annually, many of them from the United Kingdom and Germany, and there was a new emphasis on attracting tourists from China.

LABOUR AND TAXATION

In the mid-1970s, with the return of parliamentary democracy, trade unions became mobilized. For the next decade and a half there was a period of increased strike activity, characterized by greater militancy and expanding membership in organized labour. By the early 1990s, however, as the Greek economy became more stable and less industrial, trade union membership and bargaining power were diminished. Though not officially recognized, there are trade union factions belonging to each of the major political parties. Overall, however, union labour in Greece is primarily represented by the General Confederation of Greek Workers (Geniki Synomospondia Ergaton Ellados; GSEE). The Civil Servants' Confederation (Anotati Diikisis Enoseon Dimosion Ypallilon; ADEDY) is the next most important labour organization. Whether they belong to unions or not, Greeks in a wide variety of occupations —from physicians to public transportation workers—have shown a willingness to undertake wildcat strikes. There was widespread union opposition to the austerity measures (which included reductions in benefits and pensions) introduced by the government in response to the economic crisis that began in 2009.

Greece instituted a value-added tax (VAT) in 1987. Individual income tax is progressive, with rates as high as 45 percent at the beginning of the second decade of the 21st century.

TRANSPORTATION AND TELECOMMUNICATIONS

Only since the last half of the 20th century have all the country's villages become accessible to wheeled traffic and linked to the national electricity grid. There are no navigable rivers and only one waterway, the Korinthiakós (Corinth) Canal, which divides the Pelopónnisos from mainland Greece. Although the canal significantly shortens the sea route from the Italian ports to Piraeus (the port of Athens), it has never fulfilled the economic expectations of its builders, because of its shallow draft and narrow width. There are also major ports at Patras and Thessaloníki.

Railway construction began in the 1880s and, given the rugged terrain of the country, involved some difficult feats of engineering. Today the extensive railway

PIRAEUS

Piraeus, the main port for Athens, lies on Phaleron Bay, about 6 miles (10 km) southwest of Athens by highway. The main harbour, Kántharos (ancient Cantharus), is enclosed on the west by the small Ietionía peninsula, on the south by the main Akti peninsula (the Peraïki sector of the port), and on the east by the hill of Munychia (modern Kastélla).

In the 7th and 6th centuries BCE the Athenians used

The harbour at Piraeus, the port of Athens, on the Saronic Gulf, Greece. K. Honkanen/Ostman Agency

Phaleron Bay for mooring, since the present port was separated from the mainland by marshes. The Athenian statesman Themistocles persuaded his colleagues about 493 BCE to fortify and use Piraeus for the new Athenian fleet, though its fortifications were not completed until after 479. Soon after 460 the Long Walls from the base of Munychia to Athens were built, thereby ensuring communications between Athens and its port in the event of a siege. The street pattern of modern

Piraeus still approximates the rectangular grid designed for the new town by the architect Hippodamus of Miletus. The Spartans captured Piraeus at the close of the Peloponnesian War and demolished the Long Walls and the port's fortifications in 404. They were rebuilt under the Athenian leader Conon in 393 BCE. In 86 BCE the Roman commander Lucius Cornelius Sulla destroyed the city, and it was insignificant from that time until its revival after 1834, when Athens became the capital of newly independent Greece. In 1854–59, following the Crimean War, Piraeus was occupied by the Anglo-French fleet to forestall Greek expansionist intentions. Piraeus was bombed by the Germans in 1941 during World War II.

The modern port has been rebuilt since the bombings of World War II. It is the largest in Greece and is the centre of all sea communication between Athens and the Greek islands. Piraeus is also the terminal station for all the main Greek railways and is linked to Athens by electric railway and superhighway. The city has grown considerably since World War II, with many new factories on its outskirts (mainly for the engineering and chemical industries) as well as shipyards. There is a naval academy and an archaeological museum, with statuary and pottery from both the Greek and Roman periods. It is connected to downtown Athens by a light rail system.

system includes a narrow-gauge railway network in the Pelopónnisos. A program to modernize the railway system with the aid of EU funding commenced in the mid-1990s. Public transport in the Athens metropolitan area is heavily dependent on an often overcrowded and sometimes unreliable bus network. Much of Athens is serviced by the Metro; construction of that subway system began in the 1990s but proceeded relatively slowly, as the digging unearthed a treasure trove of antiquities. More subway lines are planned for the Metro, which is supplemented by a small suburban railroad network linking the northern suburb of Kifisiá with the port of Piraeus.

The extensive nationwide bus-and-ferry network has been augmented since the 1960s by the development of a flight network linking Athens with a few dozen domestic airports. The country's main airports are in suburban Athens and Makedonía, near Thessaloníki. International airports are found also at Alexandroúpoli (Alexandroúpolis) in Thráki and Andravída in the northwestern Pelopónnisos, while others service the country's important tourist destinations on the islands. For several decades Olympic Airlines was owned by the government and had a virtual monopoly on air travel within Greece, but in 2009 it was acquired by a private investment group. Meanwhile, several small, privately owned airlines began offering limited service, primarily within Greece.

In the early 21st century the saturation rate of cellular phone use was extremely high, with almost as many subscriptions as there were citizens.

CHAPTER 8

GREEK GOVERNMENT AND SOCIETY

Greece is a parliamentary republic. The current constitution, introduced in 1975 following the collapse of the 1967–74 military dictatorship, initially gave considerable powers to the president, but revisions to the constitution in 1986 made presidential powers largely ceremonial. The president, who is the head of state, is elected by the unicameral Hellenic Parliament (Vouli) and may serve two five-year terms.

The prime minister is the head of government and has extensive powers but must be able to command the confidence of the legislative branch. The latter, the unicameral Hellenic Parliament, consists of 300 deputies who are elected to four-year terms by direct universal vote; it has the power to revise the constitution. Voting is compulsory. A distinctive feature of the Greek electoral system has been the practice of incumbent governments amending the electoral law to suit their own political advantage. However, another round of constitutional revisions in 2001 introduced safeguards against political abuses, bringing about greater transparency in political operations.

LOCAL GOVERNMENT

The country is divided into 13 geographic diamerismata (regions), which have little administrative responsibility (though they are involved in education and tourism). These are further subdivided into departments (*nomoi*),

Physical map of Greece. Encyclopaedia Britannica, Inc.

each administered by a government-appointed prefect (*nomarkhis*). There are some 50 nomoi, plus an autonomous region and several prefectures. A government minister has special responsibility for Makedonía and Thráki, and another for the Aegean. The Greek system of government is highly centralized, and the powers of local governments are severely limited by their inability to raise revenue; decentralization was one of the platforms of the constitutional amendments of 2001.

JUSTICE

The judiciary is essentially the Roman law system prevalent in continental Europe. The two highest courts are the Supreme Court (Areios Pagos), which deals with civil and criminal cases, and the Council of State (Symvoulion Epikrateias), which is responsible for administration disputes. A Court of State Auditors has jurisdiction in a number of financial matters. A Special Supreme Tribunal deals with disputes over the interpretation of the constitution and checks the validity of parliamentary elections and referenda.

POLITICAL PROCESS

Many elements of traditional politics remain in Greece, most notably the personality-based nature of the party system. Parties are heavily dependent on the charisma of their leaders, and patronage is important at all levels.

In the early 21st century the major political parties included New Democracy (Nea Dimokratia; ND), the Panhellenic Socialist Movement (Panellinio Sosialistiko Kinima; PASOK), Syriza (Coalition of the Radical Left), and the Communist Party of Greece (Kommunistiko Komma Elladas; KKE). New Democracy, founded by the veteran conservative politician Konstantinos Karamanlis, consistently supported "neo-liberal" policies that aimed at limiting the power of the state and encouraging private initiatives and market economics.

NEW DEMOCRACY AND PANHELLENIC SOCIALIST MOVEMENT

The conservative New Democracy was founded in 1974 by Konstantinos Karamanlis, who oversaw the country's transition from military dictatorship to democracy. It generally supports greater economic liberalization, including privatization and lower taxes, and is a strong supporter of European integration.

New Democracy was from the outset dominated by Karamanlis, whose influence over the party's affairs continued to be strong even after he was elected president in 1980. Karamanlis's immense prestige as the person who had overseen the restoration of democracy helped New Democracy win a majority of the vote and nearly three-fourths of the parliamentary seats in November 1974 in the first postcoup elections. Under Karamanlis's leadership the party was strongly in favour of Greece's entry into the European Economic Community (EEC; renamed the European Community in 1993 and embedded within the European Union) and was committed to Greece's membership in the North Atlantic Treaty Organization and the country's western orientation.

The Panhellenic Socialist Movement (PASOK) was founded in 1974 as a radical Marxist-inspired party that called for the dissolution of the country's military alliances and for tighter government regulation of the economy, but since its founding it has transformed into a mainstream social democratic party.

In its early years PASOK espoused radical, class-based, socialist policies. It sought to define a socialist "Third Way" that was different from social democracy, Eurocommunism, and the socialism that existed in the Soviet bloc. PASOK strongly opposed the restoration of the monarchy and favoured strict controls of U.S. military operations in Greece, Greece's withdrawal from the North Atlantic Treaty Organization, and the renegotiation of Greece's membership in the EEC.

The PASOK retained a strong commitment to an independent foreign policy and a modified form of socialism. On the far left was the KKE, which continued to advocate Soviet-style communism.

SECURITY

The military, made up of an army, a navy, and an air force, was a major arbiter of political life during the 20th century. Greece's expenditure on defense is one of the highest in the North Atlantic Treaty Organization (NATO) but is largely motivated by its preoccupation with Turkey, the country's traditional enemy. Conscription for men is universal, and women have the right to volunteer for service.

HEALTH AND WELFARE

In the 1980s the government instituted a national health care system. Many Greek doctors train, at least partly, abroad, and they and the major hospitals meet international standards; however, Greeks often choose to travel abroad for medical care if they can afford it. The pension system in Greece is extraordinarily complex. Workers are insured under the Social Insurance Institute and the Agricultural Insurance Organization programs.

HOUSING

New housing construction accelerated at the end of the 20th century, particularly in the larger cities. Urban areas are characterized by apartment buildings. In fact, about half of all housing units in the early 21st century were apartments. Discrimination in housing in Greece was noted by international observers, who cited poor access to adequate housing and forced eviction among the Roma (Gypsies).

EDUCATION

Education has long been prized in Greece, both as an end in itself and as a means of upward social mobility. Wealthy Greeks of the diaspora have been major benefactors of schools and universities in their homeland. The state educational system is somewhat rigid, heavily centralized, and generally considered inadequate. As a consequence, many children attend private phrontistiria, institutions that tutor students outside normal school hours.

Education is free at all levels and is compulsory for children between ages 6 and 15. Nearly the entire population is literate. The oldest institutions of higher learning are the National Technical University of Athens (1836), the National and Capodistrian University of Athens (1837), and the Aristotle University of Thessaloniki (1925). The latter institution has a tradition of innovation compared with the more conservative University of Athens. There are several other universities and polytechnical schools and a school of fine arts; however, those institutions are often inadequately equipped and lack a sufficient number of admission openings to satisfy the demand for higher education. Many Greek students therefore choose to study abroad.

CHAPTER 9

GREEK CULTURAL LIFE

The important sites of Greek antiquity that first attracted aristocratic and upper-class Europeans to the Greek lands in the 18th century and which influenced architectural styles in the West continue to attract tourists from throughout the world. Excavated sites such as the supposed tomb of Philip II of Macedon at Verghina, the Pompeii-like remains at Akrotíri on the island of Thíra, and the Minoan palace at Zákros on Crete are a few examples of a remarkably rich heritage from antiquity that has still not been fully explored. Since the beginning of the 20th century, awareness has grown of the architectural and artistic influence of the Byzantine Empire on historic Greek churches, frescoes, mosaics, and icons. Recognized too is not only a minor renaissance of Greek art and culture during the many centuries under Venetian and western European rule (c. 1204–1669) but also the contributions of Greeks to the greater Renaissance of Italy. The Renaissance in Greece—and in Crete in particular—produced handsome buildings, frescoes, and icons as well as poetry and drama; examples of these include the Venetian Loggia in Iráklion, the paintings of Michael Damaskinos (Michail Damaskenos; flourished late 16th century), the romantic-epic poem *Erotocritos* by Vitséntzos Kornáros, and the pageant-wagon drama *Abraham and Isaac*. In addition, Greek scholars, translators, and printers of the period introduced the classics to western Europe.

Less known to foreigners but highly valued by Greeks today is the culture that emerged in the 19th century, both popular and high, as Greeks struggled to establish their new nation-state and language. They took pride in their traditional lore and poems, especially their "brigand songs," which celebrated defiance of their oppressors, while such writers as Yannis Psicháris, Andréas Ioannídis Kalvos, Dhionísios Solomós, and Alexandros Papadiamándis helped to forge a new Greek identity—one that now took pride in prevailing across centuries against foreign occupiers, in preserving the demotic language and popular customs, and in reasserting Greece's place in the history of Western civilization. Greeks celebrate their winning of independence from the Ottoman Empire with a national holiday on March 25.

DAILY LIFE AND SOCIAL CUSTOMS

In the hot summers, social life in Greece tends to be outdoors. In small towns and villages the tradition of the volta continues, when at sundown much of the population strolls up and down the main street or, on the islands, along the shore. In summer and winter much leisure time is passed in the numerous cafés and coffee shops, both of which have been traditionally a male preserve. It is also not uncommon to find in a single village one coffee shop where the adherents of a particular political party congregate. Television, the Internet, and forms of video entertainment have to some extent undermined these traditional leisure patterns.

Greek cuisine, particularly such sweets as baklava and kataifi, reflects the centuries of Turkish rule. The food in Thessaloníki—in northern Greece and part of the Ottoman Empire until 1912—in particular still reflects a strong Ottoman influence and is a testimony to the massive influx of refugees from Asia Minor in the 1920s. The traditional, healthy diet of Greek peasants in general was based on vegetables, fruit, olives, olive oil, cheese, bread, and seafood, meat being a luxury eaten only on special occasions. With the country's growing affluence, meat has come to assume a more important place in the Greek diet, "fast foods" have taken hold in the cities, and the incidence of heart disease has risen accordingly.

Greek society is noted for its strong family structure and a low crime rate. The extended family, and the obligation placed on family members to provide mutual support, is of the utmost importance. The centrality of the family has been little affected by the rise of the middle class that has been a feature of the development of Greek society since the end of World War II. During the 1980s important changes were introduced in Greek family law. Civil marriage was instituted in parallel with religious marriage, the dowry system was abolished (though marriages are still sometimes seen to some degree as economic alliances in theory), divorce was made easier, and the hitherto dominant position of the father in the family was restricted. The great majority of the country's businesses remain small, family-run enterprises. This is especially true of shipping, in which tightly knit clans of families dominate the industry. The family structure of industry acts as an impediment to modernization. The wheels of society continue to be lubricated by *mesa* (connections) and *rouspheti* (the reciprocal dispensation of favours).

The main holiday periods revolve around Easter and the Feast of Dormition (Assumption) of the Virgin in mid-August. Easter is the most important religious and family festival, with many people returning to their native villages for the traditional festivities, which include the vigil in church on Saturday evening, the lighting of the Holy Fire at midnight on Easter morning, and the roasting of whole lambs on spits for the Easter meal. August is the traditional vacation month.

THE ARTS

Against the background of this extraordinary cultural heritage, Greece enjoys a thriving artistic life. Greece has made its greatest contributions in the field of literature. Constantine Cavafy, an ethnic Greek who lived most of his life in Alexandria, Egypt, is frequently ranked among the great poets of the early 20th century. His work is suffused with an ironic nostalgia for Greece's past glories. Two Greek poets have won the Nobel Prize for Literature: George Seferis in 1963 and Odysseus Elytis in 1979. The novelist best known outside Greece is the Cretan Níkos Kazantzákis, whose *Zorba the Greek* (1946) was made into a popular film (1964). Other 20th-century Greek writers included Kostís Palamás, Angelos Sikelianós, Kostas Varnalis, Pandelís Prevelákis, Strátis Myrivílis, Yannis Ritsos, Nikephoros Vrettakos, and Nikos Gatsos. More-contemporary writers and poets include Dimitris Lyacos, Nina Rapi, Eleni Vakalo, Ersi Sotiropoulos, and Miltos Sachtouris.

A number of Greek composers have acquired an international reputation, including Nikos Skalkottas, Manos Hadjidakis, and Mikis Theodorakis, and the country has also given the world of music such notables as Dimitri Mitropoulos Maria Callas, and Gina Bachauer. Well-known Greek painters and sculptors include Nicolas Ghika, Yannis Tsarouchis, Yannis Moralis, Spyros Vassiliou, and Photis Kontoglou.

Internationally known Greek contributors to theatre and film include Karolos Koun, Melina Mercouri, Costa-Gavras, Theo Angelopoulos, and Yorgos Lanthimos. The traditional shadow puppet theatre, Karaghiozis, is now largely extinct, having been displaced by television and other leisure pursuits. There is, however, a lively Athenian theatrical tradition in which political satire plays an important part.

NÍKOS KAZANTZÁKIS

Níkos Kazantzákis (b. February 18, 1883, Iráklion, Crete, Ottoman Empire [now in Greece]—d. October 26, 1957 Freiburg im Breisgau, West Germany [now Germany]) was a Greek writer whose prolific output and wide variety of work represent a major contribution to modern Greek literature.

Kazantzákis was born during the period of revolt of Crete against rule by the Ottoman Empire, and his family fled for a short time to the Greek island of Náxos. He studied law at the University of Athens (1902–06) and philosophy under Henri Bergson in Paris (1907–09). He then traveled widely in Spain, England, Russia, Egypt, Palestine, and Japan, settling before World War II on the island of Aegina. He served as a minister in the Greek government (1945) and worked for the United Nations Educational, Scientific and Cultural Organization (UNESCO) in Paris (1947–48). He then moved to Antibes, France.

Kazantzákis's works cover a vast range, including philosophic essays, travel books, tragedies, and translations into modern Greek of such classics as Dante's *Divine Comedy* and J.W. von Goethe's *Faust*. He produced lyric poetry and the epic *Odíssa* (1938; *Odyssey*), a 33,333-line sequel to the Homeric epic that expresses the full range of Kazantzákis's philosophy.

Kazantzákis is perhaps best known for his widely translated novels. They include *Víos kai politía tou Aléxi Zormpá* (1946; *Zorba the Greek*), a portrayal of a passionate lover of life and poor-man's philosopher; *O Kapetán Mikhális* (1950; *Freedom or Death*), a depiction of Cretan Greeks' struggle against their Ottoman overlords in the 19th century; *O Khristós Xanastavrónetai* (1954; *The Greek Passion*); and *O televtaíos pirasmós* (1955; *The Last Temptation of Christ*), a revisionist psychological study of Jesus Christ. Published after his death was the autobiographical novel *Anaforá stón Gréko* (1961; *Report to Greco*). Motion pictures based on his works include *Celui qui doit mourir* (1958; "He Who Must Die," from *The Greek Passion*), *Zorba the Greek* (1964), and *The Last Temptation of Christ* (1988).

Perhaps most significant of all is the enormous influence of ancient Greek art and Greek mythology on later Western art and literature. Of countless examples that can be offered, a few should suffice to demonstrate the reach of what is known as Greek civilization. Such Greek statuary as the *kore* and the *kouros*—themselves reflecting an interaction with other cultures (particularly that of Egypt)—and later developments represented by such works as the Louvre's *Winged Victory of Samothrace* provide a major chapter in the art history of Europe and North America. In architecture, the Greek temple remains a classic form. Ancient Greek tragedies (such as Euripides' *Medea*) and comedies (such as Aristophanes' *Lysistrata*) were presented in various styles into the 21st century. One of the classic Greek tragedies—the fated marriage

The temple of Aphaea, Aíyina (Aegina), Greece. Susan McCartney/Photo Researchers

masterwork *Ulysses*. A moment's reflection can call to mind an abundance of paradigms.

CULTURAL INSTITUTIONS

Myriad venues in the capital support this theatre life, which includes productions of Western classics as well as traditional works of political satire. The numerous arts festivals held at historical sites throughout Greece during the summer months feature both native and international artists. Huge audiences are attracted to performances of ancient Greek drama staged in the theatre of Epidaurus, which dates from the 4th century BCE and whose acoustics are extraordinary; the 2nd-century-CE Roman theatre of Herodes Atticus, at the foot of the Acropolis in Athens, also

of Oedipus to his own mother, Jocasta, detailed in Sophocles' Oedipus cycle— formed a keystone of Sigmund Freud's psychoanalytic theory. Another resonant tale, Homer's *Odyssey* (8th or 9th century BCE), was the basis of Irishman James Joyce's 20th-century

ELGIN MARBLES

The Elgin Marbles are a collection of ancient Greek sculptures and architectural details in the British Museum, London, where they are now called the Parthenon Sculptures. The objects were removed from the Parthenon at Athens and from other ancient buildings and shipped to England by arrangement of Thomas Bruce, 7th Lord Elgin, who was British ambassador to the Ottoman Empire (1799–1803). The removal created a storm of controversy that exemplified questions about the ownership of cultural artifacts and the return of antiquities to their places of origin.

Elgin was a lover of art and antiquities. By his own account, he was concerned about damage being done to important artworks in the temples of Greece, then under Ottoman sway. Fearing that they would eventually be destroyed because of Turkish indifference, he asked permission of the Sublime Porte to have artists measure, sketch, and copy important pieces of sculpture and architectural detail for posterity. At length the request was granted—along with the authority "to take away any pieces of stone with old inscriptions or figures thereon."

(continued on the next page)

(continued from the previous page)

Elgin then began selecting a vast store of the treasures for shipment to England. Among these were friezes, pediment sculptures, and fragmented statues from the cella (interior chamber) walls of the Parthenon; the northeast column, an anta capital, blocks of wall crown (crown molding), including architrave and cornice, and a caryatid from the Erechtheum (a temple of Athena); and various other antiquities from Athens, Attica, and other sites.

A series of shipments took the treasures to England in 1802–12 with but one mishap—HMS *Mentor* sank in a storm off the Greek isle of Cythera in 1804, but the entire cargo was recovered. Elgin left the embassy in 1803 and arrived in England in 1806. The collection remained private for the next 10 years.

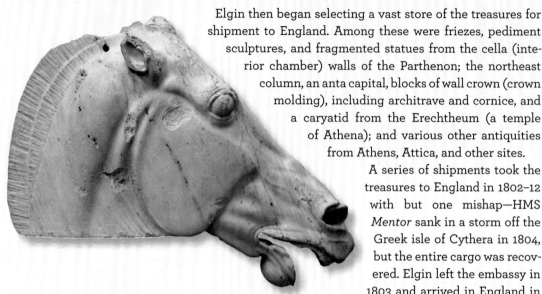

Head of a horse of Selene, the moon goddess; one of the Elgin Marbles, in the British Museum. © kmiragaya/Fotolia.

An outcry arose over the affair, and Elgin was assailed for rapacity, vandalism, and dishonesty in hauling the Grecian treasures to London. Lord Byron and many others attacked Elgin's actions in print. A select committee of Parliament was established to examine the sculpture and the possibility of acquiring it for Britain. In 1810 Elgin published a defense of his actions that silenced most of his detractors. The final shipment of the Elgin Marbles reached London in 1812, and in 1816 the entire collection was acquired from Elgin by the crown for the sum of £35,000, about half of Elgin's costs.

The Greek government has frequently demanded the return of the marbles, but the British Museum—claiming among other reasons that it has saved the marbles from certain damage and deterioration—has not acceded, and the issue remains controversial. The Acropolis Museum in Athens, which is adjacent to the ancient site, was completed in 2008; a large space in the museum is devoted to the Parthenon, and the pieces removed by Elgin are represented by veiled plaster casts.

draws large crowds and is the location for concerts at the annual Athens Festival. Live performances of orchestral music in Athens, limited in comparison with those of other European capitals, were given a major boost with the opening in 1991 of a new concert hall, the Megaro Mousikis ("Palace of Music").

The country's archaeological heritage and emphasis on the Classical past has given the state's Archaeological Service a particularly important role. Frequently working in cooperation with various foreign archaeological institutes, the service is responsible for excavating relics of the past and for running the country's museums. Far and away, the most visited of these is the National Archaeological Museum in Athens. In 2009 the new Acropolis Museum was opened to the public, with a floor set aside for the long-sought return of the Elgin Marbles from the British Museum. Access to public libraries is relatively limited, and there is no adequate national library. Distinctive of Greek intellectual life are the numerous societies devoted to the study of local and regional archaeology, history, and folklore, reflecting the strong regional loyalties of many Greeks. The country's most prestigious learned society is the Academy of Athens.

SPORTS AND RECREATION

Greece's national sport is football (soccer), and basketball has increased in popularity since the 1980s. The national basketball team won the European

ATHENS 1896 OLYMPIC GAMES

The first modern occurrence of the Olympic Games was held in Athens from April 6 to April 15, 1896. The Games were attended by as many as 280 athletes, all male, from 12 countries. The athletes competed in 43 events covering athletics (track and field), cycling, swimming, gymnastics, weightlifting, wrestling, fencing, shooting, and tennis. A festive atmosphere prevailed as foreign athletes were greeted with parades and banquets. A crowd estimated at more than 60,000 attended the opening day of competition. Members of the royal family of Greece played an important role in the organization and management of the Games and were regular spectators over the 10 days of the Olympics. Hungary sent the only national team; most of the foreign athletes were well-to-do college students or members of athletic clubs attracted by the novelty of the Olympics.

The athletics (track-and-field) events were held at the Panathenaic Stadium. The stadium, originally built in 330 BCE, had been excavated but not rebuilt for the 1870 Greek Olympics and lay in disrepair before the 1896 Olympics, but through the direction and financial aid of Georgios Averoff, a wealthy Egyptian Greek, it was restored with white marble. The ancient track had an unusually elongated shape with such sharp turns that runners were forced to slow down considerably in order to stay in their lanes. The track-and-field competition was dominated by athletes from the United States, who won 9 of the 12 events. The swimming events were held in the cold currents of the Bay of Zea. Two of the four swimming races were won by Alfréd Hajós of Hungary. Paul Masson of France won three of the six cycling events.

(continued on the next page)

(continued from the previous page)

The 1896 Olympics featured the first marathon. The race, conceived by Frenchman Michel Bréal, followed the legendary route of Pheidippides, a trained runner who was believed to have been sent from the plain of Marathon to Athens to announce the defeat of an invading Persian army in 490 BCE. The race became the highlight of the Games and was won by Spyridon Louis, a Greek whose victory earned him the lasting admiration of his nation.

championship in 1987, and the national football team qualified for its first World Cup finals in 1994 and won the European Championship in 2004. Mountain sports—hiking, climbing, and skiing—and hunting are other popular activities, and field hockey, baseball, and cricket are played regionally. Gymnastics is an ancient sport in Greece, as is athletics (track and field). Competitive running and jumping events date to 776 BCE, when the first Olympic Games were held, and Athens was host to the first modern Olympics in 1896. Over a century later, the Summer Games were again mounted in Athens, in 2004, refocusing attention on Greece's impact on the world of sport.

MEDIA AND PUBLISHING

During the 1980s traditional newspaper proprietors were to an extent displaced by new entrepreneurs, and most newspapers became tabloids. The circulation of morning papers declined while that of evening papers increased. Leading newspapers include *Ekathimerini* ("Daily"), *To Vima* ("Tribune," which moved to online and Sunday-only print publication in the wake of the 2009 economic crisis), and *Ta Nea* ("News"). A pair of free newspapers published in Athens, *Metro* and *City Press*, also became very popular beginning in the early 21st century. For the most part, the press tends to be partisan in its political comments. The government monopoly of television and radio broadcasting was broken in the 1980s, which gave rise to private stations. Like the print media, broadcasting is uncensored, particularly in its handling of political issues. Greece is home to scores of FM and AM radio stations and a few dozen television stations. By the early 21st century nearly half of all Greeks had Internet access.

CHAPTER 10

GREECE DURING THE BYZANTINE PERIOD (C. 300 CE–1453)

The geophysical structure of Greece played a significant role in shaping its pre-Classical and Classical history and continued to be influential into the medieval period, for, in spite of the administrative unity and relative effectiveness of the fiscal and military administration of the later Roman and Byzantine states, these still had to function in a geophysical context in which communications were particularly difficult. The southern Balkan Peninsula has no obvious geographic focal point. The main cities in the medieval period were Thessalonica (Modern Greek: Thessaloníki; historically, also called Salonika) and Constantinople, yet these were peripheral to the peninsula and its fragmented landscape. The degree of Byzantine political control during the Middle Ages is clearly reflected in this. In the largely inaccessible Rhodope (Rodópi) Mountains, as well as in the Pindus (Píndos) Mountains, state authority, whether Byzantine or Ottoman, always remained a rather distant factor in the lives of the inhabitants.

The relationship between this landscape of mountains, gulf-indented coasts, and valleys on the one hand and the sea on the other is fundamental to the cultural as well as to the political and the military history of Greece. The sea surrounds Greece except along its northern border; the extended coastline, including such gulfs as those of Corinth (Korinthiakós) and Thessalonica, which penetrate deep into the interior, has served as a means of communication with surrounding areas to the extent that even interior districts of the Balkans often share in the Mediterranean cultural world. The sea was also a source of danger: seaborne access from the west, from the south, or from the northeast via the Black Sea made Greece and the Peloponnese (Pelopónnisos) particularly vulnerable to invasion and dislocation.

LATE ROMAN ADMINISTRATION

At the beginning of the 4th century the regions comprised by the modern state of Greece were divided into eight provinces: Rhodope, Macedonia, Epirus (Ípeiros) Nova, Epirus Vetus, Thessaly (Thessalía), Achaea, Crete (Kríti), and the Islands (Insulae). Of the eight provinces, all except Rhodope and the Islands were a part of the larger diocese of Moesia, which extended to the Danube River in the north. (The word *diocese* originally referred to a governmental area governed by a Roman imperial vicar. The secular diocese was subdivided into provinces, each with its own governor.) Rhodope belonged to the diocese of Thrace (Thráki), while the Islands were classed as part of the diocese of Asiana, consisting of the westernmost provinces of Asia Minor. By the early years of the 5th century, administrative readjustments had divided the older diocese of Moesia into two sections, creating in the north the diocese of Dacia and in the south that of Macedonia, made up of the provinces of Macedonia I and II, with Epirus Novus and Epirus Vetus, Thessaly, Achaea, and Crete. Further changes during the middle of the 6th century resulted in the establishment of a military command known as the *quaestura exercitus*, a zone made up of the Islands and Caria, from the diocese of Asiana, together with the province of Moesia II on the Danube; it was designed as a means of providing for the armies based along the northern frontier in regions that were too impoverished or devastated to adequately support them.

In turn, these diocesan groups were parts of larger administrative units: the *praetorian prefectures*. Most of the Greek provinces were in the praetorian prefecture of Illyricum, except Rhodope, which, as a province of the diocese of Thrace, was in the prefecture of Oriens, as were the Islands. This pattern was radically altered by the developments of the 7th century.

Some of the ancient names for the regions of Greece disappeared from everyday use. However, many continued to be used in literary and administrative contexts, especially in the administration of the church, or were revived by classicizing writers of the late Byzantine period. Thus, Aitolia, Akarnania, Achaea, Arcadia (Arkadía), and Lakedaimon were used in the 13th century and after. Similarly, in central Greece, Boeotia (Voiotía), Euboea (Évvoia), and Thessaly all survived but in different contexts. Typical of their history is Euboea, which was so called until the 8th century, after which it was referred to variously as Chalkis or Euripus. Western writers after 1204 identified it as Negroponte ("Black Bridge," after the bridge connecting it to the mainland), although the Byzantines also called it Euboea. The names Epirus and Macedonia never dropped out of regular use. However, many new names were also coined during the Byzantine period; these tended to be geographic descriptions (such as Strymon [Strimón] or Boleron) used for both provincial and administrative divisions as well as to describe regions with a particular ethnic composition—for example, Vlachia in southern Thessaly.

THE EVOLUTION OF BYZANTINE INSTITUTIONS

As in other parts of the Roman world, the function of cities in the administrative structure of the state underwent a gradual evolution from the 3rd century on as the central government found it increasingly necessary to intervene in municipal affairs in order to gain revenues. This need for intervention developed when the vitality of cities became eroded as a result of a range of factors, notably the economic damage to urban infrastructures that accompanied the civil wars and barbarian inroads of the 3rd century. The so-called "decline" of the curial order (the strata of local government officials known as decurions), caused by the weakening of the fiscal and economic independence of many towns by the tendency of urban elites to avoid municipal obligations, also played a role. Finally, in the eastern parts of the empire, the transformation of Byzantium into Constantinople as a new

imperial capital in 330 had important results for patterns of internal trade and commerce as well as for social relations between provincial elites and the state. Nevertheless, the cities of the southern Balkans were able to survive the raids and devastation of both Goths and Huns in the 4th and 5th centuries, and there is no evidence that cities ceased to carry on their function as centres of market activity, local administration, and social life. Those cities that were artificial, or purely administrative creations of the Roman state, were the first to suffer, and, under difficult conditions, they generally disappeared. On the other hand, the state—through its regional and central military administration—also appears to have been involved in promoting different types of smaller defended urban centres, which were better adapted to these conditions.

In the 7th century a series of developments combined to further promote what was already in the process of becoming a radically different pattern of settlement and administration. In the first place, the results of the long-term developments already referred to, in terms of both social and economic stability, were factors. In particular, the municipal landowning elites transferred their attention—especially with respect to investment in the imperial system—away from their local cities to the imperial capital. In the second place, the economic disruption brought about by the infiltration of large numbers of Slav settlers and immigrants was exacerbated by the devastation and insecurity

BYZANTINE EMPIRE

At its peak, the Byzantine Empire covered southeastern and southern Europe and western Asia. It began as the city of Byzantium, which had grown from an ancient Greek colony founded on the European side of the Bosporus. The city was taken in 330 CE by Constantine I, who refounded it as Constantinople. The area at this time was generally termed the Eastern Roman Empire. The fall of Rome in 476 ended the western half of the Roman Empire, and the eastern half continued as the Byzantine Empire, with Constantinople as its capital. The eastern realm differed from the west in many respects: heir to the civilization of the Hellenistic era, it was more commercial and more urban. Its greatest emperor, Justinian (reigned 527–565), reconquered some of western Europe, built the Hagia Sophia, and issued the basic codification of Roman law. After his death the empire weakened. Though its rulers continued to style themselves "Roman" long after Justinian's death, "Byzantine" more accurately describes the medieval empire. The long controversy over iconoclasm within the eastern church prepared it for the break with the Roman church. During the controversy, Arabs and Seljuq Turks increased their power in the area. In the late 11th century, Alexius I Comnenus sought help from Venice and the pope; these allies turned the ensuing Crusades into plundering expeditions. In the Fourth Crusade the Venetians took over Constantinople and established a line of Latin emperors. Recaptured by Byzantine exiles in 1261, the empire was now little more than a large city-state. In the 14th century the Ottoman Turks began to encroach. Their extended siege of Constantinople ended in 1453, when the last emperor died fighting on the city walls and the area came under Ottoman control.

caused by the wars between the empire and the Avars, a Turco-Mongol confederacy that was able, from the 560s to the 630s, to harness the resources of those peoples in the plains of Hungary and in the Balkans to launch a series of extremely damaging and disruptive attacks on the Eastern Empire. Although the disruptions of the earlier invasions of the Huns and the Goths may have been as damaging in the short term, the Balkans were by this time suffering from the cumulative effects both of two centuries of constant insecurity and warfare and of endemic plague, which had struck the Eastern Empire in the 540s. It is clear from the imperial legislation of the late 5th and early 6th centuries dealing with the Danubian provinces and with Thrace, as well as from the archaeological record, that the final results of this economic disruption were to bring about the abandonment of the traditional pattern of urban economies. Even the construction of churches, which had experienced a certain efflorescence during the 6th century, virtually ceased in the 7th century. Secular construction also stopped, an extended process of ruralization of settlement and of economic life took place, and new populations penetrated far into the Peloponnese. The extent to which these new settlers replaced, or were able to live alongside, the indigenous population remains unclear.

As a consequence of these changes, the traditional administration collapsed, chiefly because the government at Constantinople could control only the coastal plains and some river valleys. The cities that remained in imperial hands, such as Corinth (Kórinthos) and Thessalonica (Thessaloníki), for example, were well-defended fortresses or had access to the sea, whence they could be supplied. Inland, tribal groupings and chieftaincies (*sklaviniai*) dominated many districts, and, while it appears that the empire claimed political sovereignty over such regions, it was rarely able to make this effective or to extract regular revenues, although tributes were obtained at times. The *sklaviniai*, however, did not control the entire inland region; there were many areas in which the indigenous population and the traditional patterns of local social structure and political organization may have survived and where imperial authority may have been recognized. The evidence is too sparse to draw definite conclusions.

Evidence for the degree of Byzantine control over the area is reflected dimly in the lists of signatories to ecclesiastical councils (especially those of 680 at Constantinople and of 787 at Nicaea [modern İznik, Turkey]) and in the various lists of bishoprics (*Notitiae episcopatuum*). From these it is clear that ecclesiastical administration in the south, especially in the Peloponnese, had suffered considerably. Many bishoprics were abandoned and had ceased to exist. At the council of 680 only 4 bishops from this region (Athens, Corinth, Lakedaimon, and Árgos) and 12 from Macedonia attended; what is believed to be a 7th-century episcopal list (the *Pseudo-Epiphanios*) records the names of only 5 metropolitan bishops from Greece, mostly from the north.

Administratively, those districts that remained under Byzantine control were organized from the later 7th century onward into the military province, or theme (Greek: *thema*), of Hellas, under its general (*strategos*). The theme initially encompassed only the easternmost parts of central Greece but gradually included parts of Thessaly and, possibly, of the Peloponnese, although in the latter case only the coastal regions were involved.

The islands of the Aegean remained largely in Byzantine hands. In late antiquity they had been relatively heavily populated, the larger ones among them—especially Lemnos (Límnos) and Thasos (Thásos) in the north—being well-known sources of agricultural produce. Arab piracy and raiding from the later 7th century onward altered this, causing many of the smaller islands to become deserted; however, the islands recovered during the 10th century.

Byzantine fortress-towns testify to the presence of sizable rural populations needing shelter from attack; the towns also served as refuges for people from the mainland fleeing Avar, Slav, or Bulgar raids. Administratively, in the second half of the 7th century they formed a component of the districts allotted to the naval theme (in the original sense of the term—an "army") of the Karabisianoi (Greek: karabos, a light ship), which represented the rump of the quaestura exercitus (the Roman military command comprising the Islands, Caria, and Moesia II). During the first half of the 8th century this command appears to have been subdivided to form the naval themes of the Kibyrrhaiotai (including parts of western Asia Minor and named after the district and town of Kibyrrha in southwestern Asia Minor), Samos (Sámos), or the Kólpos ("Gulf") in the southern zone, and Aigaion Pelagos covering the northern districts. Further subdivisions took place in the 10th–12th centuries, so that commands of the Dodecanese (Dodekánisa) Islands or the Cyclades (Kykládes) also appear in the sources.

It must be stressed that, even though the archaeological record clearly supports the conclusion that a dramatic collapse of traditional urban society and economic relations occurred, it also gives evidence of significant regional variations. The process of change was neither uniform across Greece, nor was it always as extreme in one area as in another. The degree of access to imperial resources and the ability to maintain regular contact with the imperial government were factors that gave some areas a very different appearance from others. It is important that this be borne in mind when considering the history of the various regions of Greece in the following period.

BYZANTINE RECOVERY

The Byzantine recovery of lost provinces began toward the end of the 8th century. The emperor Nicephorus I is traditionally credited with a major role in this, although the process was certainly under way before his accession. The degree of Slavicization appears to have varied considerably. For example, it is clear that by the 10th century many districts of the Peloponnese (Pelopónnisos) were Hellenized and Christianized, yet outposts of Slavic language and culture—sometimes partly Hellenized, often independent of central imperial control—survived in the less-accessible regions until the 13th and 14th centuries and perhaps beyond. Traces of the preconquest social and political structures of the northern Peloponnese may be reflected in the story of the widow Danelis, a rich landowner whose wealth was almost proverbial in the later 9th century and who may have represented the last in a line of Christianized but semiautonomous Slavic magnates who had dominated the region around Pátrai (Patras) in Achaea. She was a sponsor of the young Basil, later Basil I.

Different parts of Greece were reconquered at different times. Epirus (Ípeiros) in the northwest was gradually placed under Byzantine military administration, which was advancing inland from the coast during the first part of the 9th century. The themes of Cephallenia (Kefallinía) and Dyrrachium (Durazzo; modern Durrës) had been established by the 830s; that of Nikopolis appeared at the end of the 9th century. The theme of the Peloponnese emerged as a separate region in 812, although it was almost certainly created before this date; that of Thessalonica (Thessaloníki) had probably been established by about 812 as well, although this remains debated; those of Strymon (Strymónas) and Boleron appeared likewise during the course of the 9th century. Crete, part of which had fallen to the Arabs in 824, would not be wholly regained by Byzantium until 961.

Ecclesiastical organization once again reflects this process. A 9th-century list of bishoprics contains 10 Greek metropolitan sees, including those of Patras and Athens, compared with the 5 that appear in earlier records. During the first half of the 8th century (in the context of the Iconoclastic Controversy, a religious controversy concerning the veneration of icons, or sacred images) the ecclesiastical provinces of the old prefecture of Illyricum, which had been subject to Rome, were withdrawn by the emperor Leo III from papal authority and placed under Constantinople, thus permitting a unified program of re-Christianization of much of this region.

As Byzantine control became firmer, and as Byzantine military and political expansion northward accelerated during the 10th and early 11th centuries, older themes were subdivided, forming a mosaic of small administrative divisions. Thus, the themes of Berroia, Drougoubiteia (clearly reflecting a Slavic tribal territory), Jericho (on the

Adriatic coast between Dyrrachion and Nikopolis), and Edessa (Édhessa) or Vodena (northwest of Thessalonica) all appeared during the period from the late 9th to the 11th century.

ECONOMY AND SOCIETY

Like other regions of the Byzantine Empire, Greece had suffered economically from the warfare of the 7th and 8th centuries. The rise of the khanate of the Bulgars, established south of the Danube after 681, whose rulers were able to exercise a hegemony over their politically fragmented Slavic neighbours, meant that warfare remained endemic and economic insecurity a factor of daily existence. However, the restoration of Byzantine military and political power from the later 8th century onward and the growth of Byzantine cultural and religious influence throughout the Balkans during the 9th and 10th centuries created a context favourable to economic and demographic recovery throughout the empire, especially in the southern Balkan region.

During the 11th and 12th centuries Greece experienced a powerful economic upswing, certainly more so than Anatolia. Cities such as Thessalonica (Thessaloníki), Thebes (Thíva), and Corinth (Kórinthos) became centres of flourishing local industries and of market exchange, rivaling the imperial capital in many respects. The silk industry that developed around Thebes was especially important. The evidence

THESSALONÍKI

Thessaloníki (formerly Salonika, historically Thessalonica), is an important industrial and commercial centre, second to Athens in population and to Piraeus as a port. It is built on the foothills and slopes of Mount Khortiátis, overlooking the delta plains of the Gallikós and Vardar rivers.

The Byzantine church of Áyios (Saint) Dimítrios, Thessaloníki (Thessalonica), Greece. © Chris Hellier/Ancient Art & Architecture Collection

Founded in 316 BCE, Thessaloníki once was the capital of the Roman province of Macedonia. As a military and commercial station on the Via Egnatia, it grew to great importance in the Roman Empire. The city also was the birthplace of Mustafa Kemal (Atatürk), the founder and first president of the republic of Turkey. Thessaloníki became the headquarters for the Ottoman Liberty Society, a faction of the Young Turk movement that initiated the Turkish revolution of 1908.

The Via Egnatia traverses the city from east to west, between the Vardar Gate and the Kalamaria Gate, respectively. A 4th-century brick and marble arch built by the emperor Galerius spans the road on the east. The upper citadel walls (built during the reign of Theodosius I, 379–395) survive with restorations. Once the second city of the Byzantine Empire after Constantinople, Thessaloníki is remarkable for its many fine Byzantine churches. The domed basilica of Ayía Sofía (early 8th century) was converted into a mosque in 1585–89. Its nave, forming a Greek cross, is surmounted by a hemispherical dome covered with a rich mosaic dating from the 9th to the 10th century. The Church of Áyios Dimítrios, the city's patron saint, is early 5th century; it was entirely reconstructed in 1926–48.

Modern Thessaloníki is the terminus of rail lines to other areas of Greece and the Balkans. The harbour was opened to navigation in 1901. The city exports chrome, manganese, and numerous raw and processed agricultural products. Thessaloníki in the 1960s became a major industrial centre with the construction of a large complex including oil refineries, petrochemical plants, and steel works.

for greater wealth, especially greater disposable wealth, in the hands of local elites is found not only in documentary sources but also in a number of endowed churches, some of which are still in existence today. Many other towns, particularly those with a harbour or shelter for ships, became flourishing centres of trade and commerce and were sought-after locations for the trading posts of the Italian merchant republics after the 11th century.

RESULTS OF THE FOURTH CRUSADE

The Fourth Crusade, called by Pope Innocent III to reconquer the Holy Land, was diverted to Constantinople. Following the Crusaders' seizure and sack of the city in 1204, the European territories of the Byzantine Empire were divided up among the Western magnates. Whereas Byzantine resistance in Asia Minor was successful, so that two independent successor empires were established (those of Nicaea and Trebizond), most of Greece was quickly and effectively placed under Frankish (Western Christian) rule. The principality of Achaea (the Morea) and the Latin duchy of the Archipelago were subject to the Latin emperor, who was the ruler of the Latin Empire (also referred to as Romania) set up in Constantinople in 1204 by the Latin (Western) Christians of the Fourth Crusade and claimed jurisdiction over the territories of the Byzantine state. A kingdom of Thessalonica was established, to whose ruler the lords of Athens and Thebes owed fidelity, while the county of Cephallenia (Kefallinía) —which, along with the islands of Ithaca (Itháki) and Zacynthus (Zákynthos), had in fact already been under Italian rule since 1194, under Matteo Orsini—was nominally subject to Venice, although it was autonomous and after 1214 recognized the prince of Achaea as overlord. Finally, the lord of Euboea (Évvoia, or Negroponte) was subject to the authority of both Thessalonica and Venice. Byzantine control remained in the form of the despotate of Epirus in the northwest, in the area around Monemvasía in the eastern Peloponnese, and in the mountain fastness of the Taïyetos in Achaea and Arcadia (Arkadía). In 1261, however, the Nicaean forces were able to recover Constantinople and put an end to the Latin Empire. The recovery of some of the territory held by Frankish rulers followed, although Monemvasía actually fell, for a while, to a Frankish force in 1248. By the end of the 13th century, parts of central Greece were once again in Byzantine hands, and the Byzantine despotate of Morea controlled much of the central and southeastern Peloponnese, but to its north the principality of Achaea remained an important Frankish power.

The history of Greece reflects very closely its geopolitical structure. This fact is particularly clear in the period following the Fourth Crusade, when the former Byzantine administrative divisions were organized into various petty states, each having its own local history and political evolution.

DESPOTATE OF EPIRUS

The so-called despotate of Epirus (ruled by a *despotēs*, or lord), which usually included Cephallenia (Kefallinía), was established by Michael I Komnenos Doukas, who established effective control after 1204 over northwestern Greece and a considerable part of Thessaly. His brother and successor Theodore was able to retake Thessalonica from the Latins in 1224, where he was crowned as emperor, thus challenging the emperor of Nicaea, who claimed imperial rule. However, in 1242 the Nicaean ruler John III Ducas Vatatzes compelled Theodore's son and successor John to abandon the title of emperor, and by 1246 Thessalonica was under Nicaean rule. In 1259 much of Epirus came under Nicaean control, but this was lost by 1264; thereafter Epirus continued to be ruled by independent despots (*despotai*) until 1318. Its sheltered geographic position, between the spine of the Pindus mountain range and the Adriatic Sea, facilitated a degree of political separatism and independence from Constantinople until the Ottoman conquest. The Byzantine emperors, however, always insisted on their rights to confer the title of *despotēs*, and for much of the 14th and 15th centuries they regarded the rulers of Epirus as rebels.

From 1318 until 1337 Epirus was ruled by the Italian Orsini family, and after a short Greek recovery it was taken by the Serbs in 1348, and Ioánnina and Árta were its main political centres. From 1366 to 1384 Ioánnina was ruled by Thomas Komnenos Palaeologus, also known as Preljubovič, the son of the caesar Gregory Preljub, who had been the Serbian governor of Thessaly under Stefan Uroš IV Dušan. He was able to assert Serbian control over northern Epirus and fought with the Albanian lords of Árta (Ghin Bua Spata and Peter Ljoša) in the south, eventually defeating them with the aid of the Ottomans. In 1382 his title of *despotēs* was confirmed by the Byzantine emperor

at Constantinople. He was assassinated late in 1384, probably by members of the local nobility who objected to his rule. His widow, the Byzantine Maria Angelina Doukaina Palaiologina, married the Italian nobleman Esau Buondelmonti, who ruled as *despotēs* until about 1411. Thereafter the despotate came under the Italian house of Tocco, whose rulers were able to recover Árta from the Albanians. But in 1430 the Ottomans took Ioánnina and in 1449 they captured Árta, and, thus, Epirus became part of the Ottoman Empire. Cephallenia was taken in 1479, but Venice seized it in 1500.

THESSALY AND SURROUNDING REGIONS

The political history of the other regions of Greece during this period is no less complex. Thessaly was ruled in its eastern parts by the Franks after 1204, while the western regions were disputed by the rulers of Epirus and Nicaea. About 1267 John I Doukas established himself as independent ruler, with the Byzantine title sebastokrator, at Neopatras, but in expanding his control eastward he came into conflict with Michael VIII, whose attacks he repelled with the assistance of the dukes of Athens and Charles I of Anjou. Venetian support, the result of a favourable trading relationship (Thessaly exported agricultural produce), helped maintain Thessalian independence until the arrival in 1309 of the Catalan Grand Company. This band of Spanish mercenaries, who originally had been hired by Andronicus II to fight the Seljuqs in Anatolia, had turned against imperial authority and established themselves in the Gallipoli peninsula. From there they moved into Greece through Thrace and Macedonia, which they plundered, and from 1318 onward they occupied the southern districts of Thessaly. The northern regions remained independent under the ruler Stephen Gabrielopoulos until 1332, and then they were taken by John II Orsini of Epirus. In 1335 Thessaly was retaken by the Byzantine Empire, and from 1348 it acknowledged the overlordship of the Serbian ruler Stefan Dušan. After his death (1355) the self-styled emperor Symeon Uroš, *despotēs* of Epirus and Akarnania, was able to seize control of both Epirus and Thessaly and rule independently following the death of Nikephoros II in 1358/59. He was succeeded by his son John, who adopted the monastic life in 1373. The caesar Alexios Angelos Philanthropenos took control, governing as a vassal of the Byzantine emperor John V, but in 1393 the conquest of Thessaly by Ottoman forces put an end to its independence.

ATHENS, THEBES, AND CORINTH

In the south Greece was divided among a number of competing political units. After 1204 the dukes of Athens (mostly of French or Italian origin) controlled much of central Greece, with their main base at Thebes. They had political interests to the north and in the Peloponnese. However, in 1311 the Catalan Grand Company established its power over the duchies of Athens and Thebes, turning out their Latin lords. Under the protection of the Aragonese king Frederick II of Sicily (three sons of whom became dukes of Athens), they dominated the region until the Navarrese Company (an army of mercenaries originally hired by Luis of Evreux, brother of Charles II of Navarre, to help assert his claim over Albania and then temporarily in the service of the Hospitallers, a military-monastic order) took Thebes in 1378 or 1379. This weakened Catalan power and opened the way for the Florentine Acciajuoli, lords of Corinth, to take Athens in 1388. The latter then ruled all three regions until their defeat at the hands of the Ottomans in the 1450s.

THE PELOPONNESE

In the Peloponnese the political rivalry between the Byzantines and the Frankish principality of Achaea dominated. The principality was at its most successful under its prince William II Villehardouin (1246–78), but in 1259 he had to cede a number of fortresses, including Mistra, Monemvasiá, and Maina, to the Byzantines. Internecine squabbles weakened resistance to Byzantine pressure, especially from the 1370s onward, when Jacques de Baux hired the Navarrese Company to fight for his claim to the principality. Upon his death in 1383, the Navarrese exercised effective political control over the Frankish territories under the commanders of the company. The last Navarrese prince, Pierre de Saint-Superan, joined the Ottomans in 1401 to raid Byzantine possessions in the southern Peloponnese; he died in 1402. He was succeeded by his widow, Maria Zaccaria, representative of an important Genoese merchant and naval family. She passed the title to her nephew Centurione II Zaccaria, who lost much of the territory to the Byzantine despotate of the Morea. In 1430 he married his daughter to the Byzantine despotēs Thomas Palaeologus, handing over his remaining lands as her dowry. From this time on, the Byzantine despotate of the Morea effectively controlled most of the Peloponnese. However, the Ottoman presence and the fall of Constantinople to Sultan Mehmed II in 1453 effectively ended this final period of Byzantine rule. The Morea resisted Ottoman conquest until 1460, when it was finally incorporated into the Ottoman Empire (a year earlier than the empire of Trebizond, which fell in 1461). All of Greece was by this time under Ottoman authority, with the exception of some of the islands, which retained a tenuous independence under Venetian or Genoese protection.

SERBIAN AND OTTOMAN ADVANCES

Byzantine power in the northern Greek regions was effectively destroyed by the expansion of the Serbian empire under Stefan Dušan, the results of which included the loss of Epirus, Thessaly, and eastern Macedonia. From the 1350s the Ottomans established themselves in Europe, taking the chief towns of Thrace in the 1360s and Thessalonica in 1387. Apart from the Despotate of the Morea, therefore, and certain of the Aegean isles, there remained in Greece no Byzantine imperial possessions by the beginning of the 15th century.

THE ISLANDS

A particularly complex picture is represented by the islands, which were a focus for the activities of the Seljuqs and later the Ottomans, the Venetians and Genoese, and the Byzantines. Following the Fourth Crusade, much of the southern part of the Aegean came under Venetian authority, and, although Byzantine power was restored for a while in the late 13th century, Náxos (Náchos) remained the centre of the Latin duchy of the Archipelago, established in 1207 among the Cyclades by Marco Sanudo, a relative of the Venetian doge, or magistrate, with a body of plundering merchants and nobles. Initially under the overlordship of the Latin emperor at Constantinople, the duchy later transferred its allegiance to Achaea in 1261 and to Naples in 1267, although Venice also claimed suzerainty. The Sanudo family was replaced in 1383 by the Lombard Crispi family, which retained its independence until 1566. At that time the duchy was conquered by the Ottomans, although it was ruled by an appointee of the sultan until 1579, when it was properly incorporated into the state.

The remaining islands were held at different times by the Venetians, the Genoese, the Hospitallers, and the Turks. Rhodes played a particular role in the history of the Hospitallers' opposition to the Ottomans. Until the early 13th century the island had been in the hands of a succession of Italian adventurers, most of whom acknowledged the overlordship of the emperor at Nicaea. In 1308 the Hospitallers took control, having been based on Cyprus since 1291, the time of their expulsion from the Holy Land. Rhodes fell in 1523, when the Hospitallers were permitted to remove to Malta. Of the northern Aegean islands, Lemnos remained Byzantine until 1453 before coming for a while under the rule of the Gattilusi of Lésbos, whose independence of the Ottomans ended in 1462. In 1460 it was awarded to Demetrius Palaeologus, formerly despotēs of the Morea, along with the island of Thasos (the latter having come under Ottoman domination in 1455). In 1479 it was occupied by Ottoman forces and officially incorporated into the Ottoman state. Other islands had equally checkered histories. Náxos and Chíos (Khíos) fell in 1566, although complete Ottoman control was not achieved until 1715, when Tenedos, which remained under Venetian control until that year, was taken.

The Venetian fort at Iráklion (Candia), Greece. Tiers/Monkmeyer

The real exception to the Ottoman success in the Aegean, however, was Crete. Separately administered until the 820s, when it was seized by Spanish Arabs, it was conquered in 961 by the general and later Byzantine emperor Nicephoros II Phocas. After 1204 it was handed over to Boniface of Montferrat, who proceeded to sell it to Venice. Although oppressive and unpopular, Venetian rule witnessed the evolution of a flourishing Italo-Hellenic literary and political culture. After a long siege of Candia (now Iráklion) and the creation and collapse of temporary alliances between Venice and various Western powers on the one hand and the Ottomans and their supporters on the other, the island passed into Ottoman hands in 1669.

ECONOMIC AND SOCIAL DEVELOPMENTS

In spite of the political instability after 1204, Greece seems to have experienced relative prosperity in the later Byzantine period. Population expansion accompanied an increase in production as marginal lands were brought under cultivation, and trade with major and minor Italian mercantile centres flourished. Although hostility at the level of state politics was endemic, social relations between the ruling elites of Byzantine- and Latin-dominated areas were not mutually exclusive. Intermarriage was not uncommon, and a certain way of life seems to have evolved. This contrasted with the attitude of the peasantry and the ordinary population, whose perceptions were shaped by the Orthodox church, Greek or Byzantine ("Roman") identity, and hostility to the Western church and its ways. The Ottoman conquest was not seen as necessarily worse than Latin domination; in some cases, it was certainly welcomed as less oppressive.

CULTURAL CONTINUITY

The history of medieval Greece has played an important part in attempts to understand the relationship between ancient and modern Greece. The issue of the continuity between ancient and modern Greeks has been an extremely controversial one, in both scholarly and political contexts. The claim that modern Greeks are the direct cultural and biological descendants of the "ancient Hellenes" has long been a central tenet of the national ideology on which the Greek state was founded. Scholars such as the Austrian-born 19th-century German historian Jakob Fallmerayer argued that, as a result of the large Slav and Albanian invasions during the medieval period, the latter-day population of Greece could not be entirely of Greek "racial" origin. Greek scholars in such diverse disciplines as archaeology, linguistics, folklore, and history have attempted to identify "survivals" from ancient Greek culture that can still be found in its modern counterpart. While there certainly are significant similarities that demonstrate continuities in some aspects of Greek culture, there are also equally important differences that demonstrate discontinuities in other aspects of Greek culture. Unfortunately, scholarship on this issue has often been overshadowed by nationalist and romantic political agendas of Greeks and non-Greeks alike.

THE SLAVS

A large number of Slavs entered what is now Greece during the late 6th to 8th centuries. Although the evidence of place-names suggests some lasting Slavic influence in parts of Greece, it is qualified by the fact that the process of re-Hellenization that occurred from the later 8th century seems to have eradicated many traces of Slavic presence. Evidence of tribal names found in both the Peloponnese and northern Greece suggests that there were probably extensive Slavic-speaking populations in many districts, and from the 10th to the 15th century Slavic occupants of various parts of the Peloponnese appear in sources as plunderers or as fiercely independent warriors. Whereas the Slavs of the south appear to have adopted Greek, those of Macedonia and Thessaly retained their original dialects, becoming only partially Hellenophone in certain districts.

THE ALBANIANS

The origins of the Albanian-speaking population in Greece, known as Arvanites, remain uncertain. They appear to be the descendants of the Illyrian populations who withdrew into the highlands of the central Dinaric chain. Their name may originate from the valley of the Arbanon (along the Shkumbi River) in the theme of Dyrrachion (Durrës or Durazzo), in which they were first noted by outside commentators. Their language probably evolved from ancient Illyrian, which was formerly classed with the Hellenic group of Indo-European languages but was later recognized as an independent member of the latter family; it is heavily influenced by Greek, Slavic languages, Turkish, and medieval Italian. The Albanians in the 14th century began to advance into Greece's western coastal plain, where they served both Byzantine and Serbian overlords and ruled independently under various warlords and chiefly families; they were

also present in considerable numbers in Thessaly, Boeotia, Attica (Attikí), and the Peloponnese, serving as soldiers and farmers and colonizing deserted lands. Albanians arrived in large numbers in the Peloponnese during the reign of the despotēs Manuel Kantakouzenos, who brought them there to serve as soldiers and to resettle depopulated regions. The reason for their migration to these areas as well as the impact of their presence on the region's existing ethnic and linguistic structure remains debated. These early Albanian-speaking settlers constitute a group distinct from the economic migrants from Albania, who have settled in Greece in the late 20th and early 21st centuries and who are simply known as "Albanians" (Greek: Alvanoi).

THE AROMANI

The Aromani (Vlachs) played an important role in central and southern Thessaly. They have generally been identified with the indigenous, pre-Slav populations of Dacian and Thracian origin, many of whom migrated into the less accessible mountainous areas of Greece and the northern Balkan region because of the Germanic and Avar-Slav invasions and immigration of the 5th–7th centuries. The Aromani maintained a transhumant pastoral economy in those areas. Their language belongs to the so-called Macedo-Romanian group and is closely related to that known from the 13th century on as Romanian (Daco-Romanian);

it is essentially rooted in late Latin but heavily influenced by the Slavic dialects with which the Daco-Thracian populations were in regular contact. By the 11th century the Aromani are described as communities of shepherds who moved with their flocks between their winter pastures in Thessaly and summer pastures in Mount Gramoz and the Pindus range; they are found in Byzantine armies and are mentioned in many documents dealing with landholdings in northern Greece, where—as is often the case in relations between settled and nomadic populations—they were regarded as troublemakers and thieves. Byzantines were often imprecise in their use of ethnic names; the Aromani seem frequently to have been confused with the Bulgarians, through whose territory they also wandered on their seasonal routes and pasturage. A major modern debate about the role of the Aromani in the establishment of the second Bulgarian empire after 1185 continues and is strongly marked by nationalist sentiment.

EMERGING GREEK IDENTITY

As the Byzantine Empire declined, the predominant role of Greek culture, literature, and language became more apparent. For Christians of the early and middle Byzantine worlds, the terms Hellene and Hellenic generally (although not exclusively, since in certain literary contexts a classicizing style permitted a somewhat different usage) had a negative connotation, signifying pagan and non-Christian rather than "Greek." From the 12th century, however, in the context of increasing conflict with western European culture on the one hand and the encroaching Turkish powers on the other, this situation changed. Gradually a more self-consciously Greek consciousness began to develop, and a greater interest in "Hellenic" culture in a positive sense eventually evolved. Byzantines began to refer to themselves not just as "Romioi" (literally, "Roman," referring to members of the Eastern Roman [that is, Byzantine] Empire). In the decades prior to the Greek War of Independence, the Greeks began to identify themselves as "Hellenes" and assert their identity with the ancient Hellenic world. Among learned circles a deep interest in the Classical past was cultivated. While there was a powerful secularist tradition in this, culminating in the ideas of the Neoplatonic Byzantine philosopher George Gemistus Plethon, who argued for the implementation of the political-philosophical system outlined in Plato's *Republic*, it was the combination of popular Orthodoxy (and strongly anti-Western ecclesiastical sentiment) with a specifically Greek identity that shaped the Byzantines' notions of themselves in the twilight years of the empire. With the political extinction of the empire, it was the Greek Orthodox Church and the Greek-language community, in both "Greece" and Asia Minor, that continued to cultivate this identity as well as the ideology of a Byzantine imperial heritage rooted in both the Roman and the Classical Greek past.

CHAPTER 11

GREECE FROM OTTOMAN RULE THROUGH INDEPENDENCE

Constantinople fell to the Ottoman Turks on May 29, 1453. The Byzantine emperor, Constantine XI Palaeologus, was last seen fighting alongside his troops on the battlements; his death gave rise to the widely disseminated legend that the emperor had turned to marble but would one day return to liberate his people. By 1453 the Byzantine Empire had become but a pathetic shadow of its former glories.

OTTOMAN GREECE

The fall of the Byzantine Empire, a symbolic bastion of Christendom in the struggle against Islam, may have sent shock waves through Western Christendom, but the conquest was accepted with resignation by many of the inhabitants of the city; as they saw it, their plight was a consequence of the sinfulness of the Byzantine Empire. For many people, Ottoman rule and the maintenance of the integrity of the Orthodox faith were preferable to accepting the pretensions of the papacy, which was the price Western Christendom had sought to exact in return for military assistance to ward off the Turkish threat.

THE *MILLET* SYSTEM

With the conquest of the territories that had constituted the Byzantine Empire, the Ottoman sultans were faced with the problem of governing large non-Muslim populations. Christians and Jews, as "People of the Book," were afforded a considerable degree of toleration. Indeed, it was to the Ottoman Empire rather than Christian Europe that many Spanish Jews migrated following their expulsion from Spain in 1492. The Ottomans confronted the problem of the governance of these large heterodox and polyglot populations by establishing *millet*s. These were organized on the basis of religious confession rather than ethnic origin. The ruling *millet* within the empire was made up of the Muslims. Next in importance was the Orthodox Christian Rūm millet, which was often called the "Greek *millet*." Although its head, the ecumenical patriarch, was invariably of Greek origin, the term Greek *millet* was something of a misnomer, for it included not only Greeks but also Romanians, Bulgarians, Serbs, Albanians, Aromani, and substantial Arab populations who as Orthodox Christians were also members of the

Rūm *millet*. With the rise of nationalism in the 18th and 19th centuries, the non-Greek members of the Greek *millet* became increasingly resentful of the Greek stranglehold on the higher reaches of the hierarchy of the Orthodox church, through which the *millet* was administered. There were also Armenian, Jewish, Roman Catholic, and Protestant *millet*s.

The powers of the ecumenical patriarch were extensive, although there is uncertainty as to the precise nature of the privileges granted by Sultan Mehmed II to the man whom he elevated to the highest office in the church. This was Gennadios II Scholarios, a known opponent of those who, in the last years of the Byzantine Empire, had advocated union with the Western church. Patriarchal authority was considerable and extended to civil as well as to strictly religious matters. In many respects, it was greater

PEOPLE OF THE BOOK

In Islamic thought, Jews, Christians, and Zoroastrians are held to be the possessors of divine books (i.e., the Torah, the Gospel, and the Avesta), as distinguished from those whose religions are not based on divine revelations. Known as "People of the Book" (Arabic: *Ahl al-Kitāb*), they are granted special protections under Islamic law.

The Prophet Muḥammad gave many privileges to the People of the Book that were not extended to other non-Muslims. They were allowed freedom of worship; thus, during the early Muslim conquests, Jews and Christians were not forced to convert to Islam and had only to pay a special tax for their exemption from military service. Muslim authorities are responsible for the protection and well-being of the People of the Book, for, according to a saying of the Prophet, "he who wrongs a Jew or a Christian will have myself [the Prophet] as his indicter on the day of judgment." After Muḥammad's death, his successors sent strict instructions to their generals and provincial governors not to interfere with the People of the Book in their worship and to treat them with full respect.

than that enjoyed by the patriarchs in Byzantine times. The privilege of a considerable degree of autonomy in directing the affairs of the *millet* carried with it the responsibility of ensuring that its members were unshaken in their loyalty to the Ottoman Porte. At the outbreak of the War of Greek Independence in 1821, the patriarch Grigorios V was executed in reprisal, despite the fact that he had vigorously condemned the insurgents, whose efforts to create an independent Greek state he saw as a threat to his power. In the West his execution was seen as an act of mindless barbarity. In the eyes of the Ottomans, however, Grigorios had failed to carry out his fundamental obligation to ensure that the adherents to the Orthodox faith remained loyal to the sultan.

DISADVANTAGES FOR NON-MUSLIMS

In keeping with Islamic tradition, members of the Greek *millet* enjoyed a considerable degree of autonomy in conducting their religious affairs. They were, however, at a disadvantage in a number of ways in comparison with members of the ruling Muslim *millet*. A Christian was not allowed to bear arms and was disbarred from military service (although this latter disability was in many ways a privilege) in exchange for paying a special tax, the haradj. In a court of law, a Muslim's word was always accepted over that of a Christian, although disputes between Christians were generally settled in courts under the control of their own *millet*. A Christian could not marry a Muslim woman, and there was a strict prohibition against renouncing Islam. Those Christians who had embraced Islam and then reverted back to Christianity were, until well into the 19th century, punished by death. These "neomartyrs," however, helped sustain the faith of the Orthodox populations during the centuries of Ottoman rule.

The most serious disability to which Christians were subject, until the practice died out toward the end of the 17th century, was the Janissary levy (paidomazoma). Christian families in the Balkans were required, at irregular intervals, to deliver to the Ottoman authorities a given proportion of their most intelligent and handsome male children to serve, after being forcibly converted to Islam, as elite troops or civil servants. Inevitably, the levy was much feared, but those who were conscripted frequently rose to high office and were sometimes able to help their relatives or their native villages. There is evidence that some Muslim families sought to pass off their children as Christian in the hope that they would be included in the levy and would thus be able to better their prospects. Under such pressures there were numerous instances of Christian conversion to Islam on both an individual and a mass basis; such conversions were particularly prevalent in the 17th century. The conversions were often only nominal, however, and these crypto-Christians secretly practiced the rituals of their former faith.

RESISTANCE TO OTTOMAN RULE

During much of the four centuries of the "Tourkokratia," as the period of Ottoman rule in Greece is known, there was little hope that the Greeks would be able to free themselves by their own efforts. There were sporadic revolts, such as those that occurred on the mainland and on the islands of the Aegean following the defeat of the Ottoman navy in 1571 by Don John of Austria, the short-lived revolt launched by Dionysius Skylosophos in Epirus in 1611, and the abortive uprising in the Peloponnese in 1770 at the time of the Russo-Turkish War of 1768–74. These uprisings had little chance of success, but during the Tourkokratia there was some armed resistance against the Turks by the klephts (social bandits or brigands). In their banditry the klephts did not distinguish between Greek and Turk, but their attacks on such manifest symbols of Ottoman authority as tax collectors led to their being seen by Greeks in later periods as acting on behalf of the Greeks against Ottoman oppressors. Certainly, they are viewed in this light in the corpus of klephtic ballads that emerged, extolling the bravery and military prowess of the klephts as well as their heroic resistance to the Ottomans.

In an effort to counter the plunderous activities of the klephts and to control the mountain passes that were their favoured areas of operation, the Ottomans established a militia of armatoloi. Like the klephts, these were Christians, and the distinction between klepht and armatolos was a narrow one. One day's klepht might be the next day's armatolos. The existence of such armed formations meant that when the War of Greek Independence broke out in 1821, the klephts formed an invaluable reserve of military talent.

BELIEF IN DIVINE INTERVENTION

Greek aspirations for freedom were largely sustained by a collection of

KLEPHTIC BALLADS

Songs and poems extolling the adventures of the Klephts, Greek nationalists living as outlaws in the mountains during the period of Ottoman rule over Greece, the Kleptic ballads contain some of the most beautiful and vivid verse in Modern Greek. The songs, mainly from the 18th century, are an entirely spontaneous poetry, composed in popular language and in 15-syllable verse, rhymed and unrhymed. They are pervaded with the spirit of the forests and the mountains and, like much Greek popular poetry, personify trees, rocks, and rivers. Even the mountains praise the prowess of the Klephts, bewail their deaths, and comfort the disconsolate wives and mothers. Klephtic ballads have been a source of inspiration and rejuvenation to Modern Greek poetry and to Greek nationalism.

prophetic and messianic beliefs that foretold the eventual overthrow of the Turkish yoke as the result of divine rather than human intervention. Such were the oracles attributed to the Byzantine emperor Leo VI (the Wise), which foretold the liberation of Constantinople 320 years after its fall—in 1773. Many believed in this prophecy, for its fulfillment coincided with the great Russo-Turkish War of 1768–74, one of the periodic confrontations between the two great regional powers. The Russians were the only Orthodox power not under foreign domination, and they were widely identified with the legendary xanthon genos, a fair-haired race of future liberators from the north. The Russians were seen as forming part of a commonwealth, which linked the various parts of the Orthodox Christian world with its common centres of pilgrimage in the monastic republic of Mount Athos (forming one of the three fingers of the Chalcidice Peninsula) and Jerusalem.

THE ROLE OF THE ORTHODOX CHURCH

The Orthodox church was the only institution on which the Greeks could focus. Through the use of Greek in the liturgy and through its modest educational efforts, the church helped to some degree to keep alive a sense of Greek identity, but it could not prevent Turkish (which was written with Greek characters) from becoming the vernacular of a substantial proportion of the Greek population of Asia Minor and of the Ottoman capital itself.

The Orthodox church, however, fell victim to the institutionalized corruption of the Ottoman system of government. The combination of civil and religious power in the hands of the ecumenical patriarchate and the upper reaches of the hierarchy prompted furious competition for high office. The Ottomans encouraged such behaviour, and it soon became the norm that, on every occasion when a new patriarch was installed, a huge peshkesh, or bribe, would be paid to the grand vizier, the sultan's chief minister. Despite the fact that, in theory, a patriarch was elected for life, there was a high turnover in office, and some even held the office more than once. Grigorios V was executed by the Ottomans in 1821 during his third patriarchate, while during the second half of the 17th century Dionysius IV Mouselimis was elected patriarch at least five times. It was this kind of behaviour that prompted an 18th-century Armenian chronicler to taunt the Greeks that they changed their patriarch more frequently than they changed their shirt.

Bribes had to be paid to secure offices at all levels, and these could be recouped only through the taxes placed on the Orthodox faithful as a whole. The clergy's reputation for rapacity led to the growth of popular anticlericalism, particularly among the small nationalist intelligentsia that emerged in the course of the 18th century. The anonymous author of that fiery nationalist polemic the "Ellinikhí Nomarkhía" ("Hellenic Nomarchy") in 1806 was a bitter critic of the sloth and self-indulgence of the higher clergy, while Adamántios Koraïs, the intellectual mentor of the national revival, though careful to steer between what he termed the Scylla of superstition and the Charybdis of atheism, condemned the obscurantism of the clergy. What particularly incensed Koraïs and his kind was the willingness of the Orthodox hierarchy to identify its interests with those of the Ottoman authorities. However, the views of men such as Anthimos, the patriarch of Jerusalem, who argued in 1798 that the Ottoman Empire was part of the divine dispensation granted by God to protect Orthodoxy from the taint of Roman Catholicism and of Western secularism and irreligion, were not unusual.

TRANSFORMATION TOWARD EMANCIPATION

During the 16th and 17th centuries the Greeks were mostly concerned with survival. In the course of the 18th century, however, a number of changes occurred both in the international situation and in Greek society itself that gave rise to hopes that the Greeks might themselves launch a revolt against Ottoman authority with some promise of success.

SIGNS OF OTTOMAN DECLINE

By the end of the 17th century, the prolonged process of Ottoman decline was clearly under way. The failure of the Siege of Vienna in 1683 signaled the retreat of the Ottomans in the European provinces of the empire; the military triumphs of earlier centuries gave way to pressure

ALI PAŞA TEPELENË

Ali Paşa Tepelenë (b. 1744, Tepelenë, Albania, Ottoman Empire—d. February 5 [January 24, Old Style], 1822, Janina, Ottoman Empire [now Ioánnina, Greece]) was an Albanian brigand who, by murder and intrigue, became pasha, or provincial governor, of Janina from 1788. Known as the Lion of Janina, he extended his capricious rule within the Ottoman Empire over much of Albania and Macedonia, Epirus, Thessaly, and the Morea.

His father, Veli, bey of Tepelenë, died a poor man when Ali was 14. His mother, Khamco, formed a brigand band to restore the political and material fortunes of the family, and Ali became a notorious brigand leader. After service with the pasha of Negroponte (Euboea), he joined the wealthy pasha of Delvino, whose daughter he married in 1768. Becoming lieutenant to the derbend-pasha of Rumelia, he policed the highroads, enriched himself, and sent presents to Constantinople. At length he was rewarded with the pashalik of Trikkala and, after a series of murders and intrigues, obtained that of Janina. His son Veli took over Trikkala and later the Morea, while another son, Mukhtar, became pasha of Lepanto. Though constantly thwarted by the Christian Souliots, whom he finally subdued in 1803, Ali obtained control of the Gulf of Arta and took the ports of Butrinto, Preveza, and Vonitsa. He also gained control of the pashaliks of Elbasan, Delvino, Berat, and Valona (Vlore).

All this time, by murders and extortions, he increased his wealth and, by intriguing with Greeks and Albanians, extended his authority over beys and townships. Though appointed viceroy of Rumelia, he repeatedly failed to carry out the orders of the Ottoman sultan, to whom he sent plausible excuses and many presents. Indeed, he acted as an independent sovereign and was treated as such by the British and French, with whom he intrigued, hoping to establish Janina as a sea power. By 1819 the sultan, Mahmud II, who intended to centralize the government of his empire, was determined to remove Ali and sanctioned his assassination. Ali tried to save himself by his old methods of murder, intrigue, and extortion but, deserted by his sons and allies, was finally shot down.

In Ali's time, Janina was the foremost centre of Greek culture, for Ali employed Greeks and founded Greek schools. His court was one of barbarous refinement, and even the liberated Greeks looked back upon him with some respect.

on their empire from the Austrians, the Russians, and the Persians. The Russian threat culminated in the 1768–74 war with Turkey, and the Russians subsequently claimed the right to exercise a protectorate over all the Orthodox Christians of the Ottoman Empire on the basis of their interpretation of the terms of the peace settlement with the Ottoman Empire by the Treaty of Küçük Kaynarca.

Forced onto the defensive, the empire lost territory, and the control of the Ottoman Porte over its enormous provinces weakened. In both European and Asiatic Turkey, provincial warlords supplanted the authority of the sultan. The example of successful defiance of the Porte carried out by powerful satraps such as Ali Paşa Tepelenë, the Muslim Albanian who ruled over a large portion of mainland Greece, gave encouragement to Greek nationalists because it demonstrated that the empire was no longer the invincible monolith it had once been.

THE PHANARIOTES

Of critical importance to the ultimate success of the national movement was the transformation that Greek society was to undergo during the course of the 18th century. Significant among these developments was the rise to power and influence of the Phanariotes, a small caste of Greek (and Hellenized Romanian and Albanian) families who took their collective name from the Phanar, or Lighthouse, quarter of Constantinople, the home of the ecumenical patriarchate. The roots of their ascendancy can be traced to the Ottomans' need for skilled negotiators as the power of their empire declined. No longer in a position to dictate peace terms to their vanquished enemies, they now had to rely on diplomats skilled in negotiation who might mitigate the consequences of military defeat, and these were drawn from the Phanariotes. From

1699, when the Treaty of Carlowitz with the Habsburg monarchy was signed, to 1821, the year of the outbreak of the War of Greek Independence, Phanariote grandees monopolized the post of chief interpreter to the Porte. This was a more important post than it appeared, for its holder bore considerable responsibility for the conduct of foreign policy. Similarly, Phanariotes were invariably interpreters to the *kapudan pasha*, the admiral of the Ottoman fleet. Again their powers were wider than the title suggests: these Phanariotes, in effect, acted as governors of the islands of the Aegean archipelago, whose Greek inhabitants were a potential source from which to draw men for service in the Ottoman fleet.

The most important posts held by Phanariotes were those of *hospodar*, or prince, of the Danubian principalities of Moldavia and Wallachia. Phanariotes ruled these potentially rich provinces as the viceroys of the sultans, and their luxurious courts in Jassy (now Iași, Romania) and Bucharest copied on a lesser scale the splendour of the imperial court in Constantinople. Just as there was furious and corrupt jockeying for high office in the Orthodox church, the appointment of the *hospodars* was also accompanied by intrigue and corruption. The average tenure in office of a Phanariote *hospodar* was less than three years. Because they needed to make up for their expenditures on bribes, *hospodars* acquired a somewhat justified reputation for greed and oppression. Some *hospodars* displayed

an enlightened interest in legal and land reform; most acted as patrons of Greek culture, education, and printing. The princely academies attracted teachers and pupils from throughout the Orthodox commonwealth, and there was some contact with intellectual trends in Habsburg central Europe. For the most part, the Phanariotes were too closely joined to the Ottoman system of government, of which they were major beneficiaries, to play a significant part in the emergence of the Greek national movement. Their interests, however, coincided with the maintenance of the Ottoman status quo, and they provided a pool of individuals with experience in diplomacy and politics when armed struggle erupted in 1821.

THE MERCANTILE MIDDLE CLASS

The single most important development in the Greek world during the 18th century was the emergence of an entrepreneurial, prosperous, and far-flung mercantile middle class, which played a major role in the economic life of the Ottoman Empire and elsewhere. Discouraged from investing their capital within the empire by the arbitrariness and rapacity of the state, these Greek merchants played an active role in developing commerce in Hungary and Transylvania, newly acquired by the Habsburg monarchy, and in southern Russia, where Empress Catherine II (the Great) encouraged them to settle after Russia's borders had extended to the

Black Sea. Greek became the common language of Balkan commerce as these merchants challenged the existing hold of British, French, and Dutch merchants on the import-export trade of the empire, importing Western manufactured goods and colonial produce and exporting raw materials. Greek merchant communities, or *paroikies*, each with its own church, were established through much of central Europe, on the Mediterranean coast, in southern Russia, and even as far away as India.

Paralleling this development, a substantial merchant marine, based on the three "nautical" islands of Hydra (Ídhra), Spétsai (Spétses), and Psará, came into existence. This merchant marine prospered from running the continental blockade imposed by Great Britain during the period of the French Revolution and Napoleonic Wars. The existence of a reservoir of trained sailors proved to be an inestimable advantage once the war of independence broke out, and Greek fire ships (combustibles-laden ships set afire and guided toward the enemy) became a formidable weapon against the cumbersome ships of the Ottoman fleet.

The emergence of a mercantile middle class had a number of important consequences. Greeks were brought into contact with the ordered societies of western Europe, in which the state encouraged commerce. They compared this state of affairs with the prevailing one in the Ottoman Empire, where the absence of the rule of law and general

The port of Ýdra (Hydra), Greece. George Holton/ Photo Researchers

arbitrariness militated against the generation and retention of capital. Most of the merchants were, like the Phanariotes, too much a part of the status quo to give active encouragement to the national movement and thus potentially threaten their newfound prosperity. Indirectly they made a major contribution to the emerging national movement, for it was their wealth that provided the material basis for the intellectual revival that was such a significant feature of the late 18th and early 19th centuries. Impelled by a sense of local patriotism which had always been strong in the Greek world, they endowed schools and libraries. It was no accident that the three most important schools-cum-colleges in the Greek world on the eve of the war of independence were situated in Smyrna (now İzmir, Turkey), Chíos, and Ayvalık (on the coast of Asia Minor opposite the island of Lésbos), all three major centres of Greek commerce.

THE INTELLECTUAL REVIVAL

A significant number of schoolteachers studied, with the financial backing of their merchant benefactors, in the universities of western Europe, particularly those of Italy and the German states. There they came under the influence of the ideas of the Enlightenment and encountered the fervent nationalist doctrines emanating from the French Revolution. They became aware of the reverence with which the language and culture of ancient Greece were beheld throughout Europe. This realization kindled in them a consciousness of their own past, a recognition of being the heirs to this same civilization and of speaking a language that had changed remarkably little in the two and a half millennia since the time of Pericles. During the 50 years or so before 1821, a veritable flood of books on the language, literature, and history of the ancient Greek world was published for a Greek readership, though most of it was outside the Greek domains.

A leading role in the rediscovery of the past was played by Adamántios Koraïs. A native of Smyrna, where he was born in 1748, Koraïs sought, unsuccessfully, to establish himself as a merchant in Amsterdam. After studying medicine at the University of Montpellier, he moved to Paris in 1788, where he soon experienced the French Revolution. The main interest of his life, however, was Classical philology, of which he became one of the foremost scholars in Europe of his day. He devoted his years in Paris to the study of this subject as well as to inspiring in his compatriots an appreciation of their Classical ancestry (until his death in 1833). With the help of a family of rich merchants of Ioánnina (Janina), he published a whole series of editions of Classical authors, which he prefaced with appeals to his compatriots to cast off their Byzantine ignorance by reviving the glories of the ancient world and by imitating the French—the people of modern Europe who, in his estimation, most resembled his Classical ancestors. His panacea for the degraded condition of the Greeks was education; it would enable them to free themselves from the double yoke of the Ottoman Turks and the Orthodox church.

The practice of naming children and ships after the heroes of ancient Greece, a custom dating from the first decade of the 19th century, is one example of what is sometimes referred to as an obsession with antiquity on the part of the small nationalist intelligentsia. Another is the vigorous debate that got under way on the appropriate form of language to be used in a regenerated Greece. Some advocated using the spoken language, the Demotic, as the language of educated discourse. Others favoured the Katharevousa, or purified Greek, which would render it more akin to Attic Greek. Still others, such as Koraïs, advocated a middle path.

Much of the intellectual revival of the half century or so before 1821 took place in the Greek communities of the diaspora, and the nationalist enthusiasms of the

ATTIC GREEK

With the ascendance of the Athenian empire over the course of the 5th century BCE, the Attic Greek dialect became the most prestigious of the Greek dialects and as a result was adopted later as the standard language by the Macedonian kings. Moreover, it became in Hellenistic times the language of the Macedonian rulers in the Middle East and Egypt. This later phase of Attic is called Koine, a dialect common to all Greeks.

In literature, Attic is the dialect of Athenian comedy and, interspersed with Doric lyric elements, of tragedy. In the second half of the 5th century BCE, it also became the dialect of Greek prose, not only for such Athenian writers as Thucydides, Xenophon, Plato, Lysias, Isocrates, and Demosthenes but also for foreigners such as the orator and Sophist Gorgias of Leontini (Sicily). During the Roman period, prose writers such as Plutarch and Lucian were Atticists: they preferred to use the classical Attic dialect of the 5th and 4th centuries BCE, rather than the spoken Koine of their own time.

intelligentsia left the great mass of the peasantry, most of whom were illiterate, largely unmoved. The elites of preindependent Greek society—the higher clerics, the wealthy merchants, the Phanariotes, and the *kodjabashis*, the wealthy provincial notables, whose lifestyle sometimes led to their being derisively referred to as "Christian Turks"—were mostly supporters of the status quo under the Ottomans. Whatever the faith Koraïs pinned on education, cultural revival by itself was not going to remove the oppressive Turks.

FROM INSURGENCE TO INDEPENDENCE

Toward the end of the 18th century, Rigas Velestinlis (also known as Rigas Pheraios), a Hellenized Vlach from Thessaly, began to dream of and actively plan for an armed revolt against the Turks. Rigas, who had served a number of Phanariote *hospodars* in the Danubian principalities, spent part of the 1790s in Vienna. There he had come under the influence of the French Revolution, which is apparent in a number of revolutionary tracts he had printed, intending to distribute them to help stimulate a Pan-Balkan uprising against the Ottomans. These tracts included a *Declaration of the Rights of Man* and a *New Political Constitution of the Inhabitants of Rumeli, Asia Minor, the Islands of the Aegean, and the Principalities of Moldavia and Wallachia.* The latter proposed the establishment of what basically would have been a revived Byzantine Empire, but an empire in which monarchical institutions would have been replaced by republican institutions on the French model. Rigas's insistence on the cultural predominance of the Greeks, however, and on the use of the Greek language, meant that his schemes stirred little interest among the other peoples of the Balkan Peninsula. In any case, Rigas's ambitious schemes failed. Before he had even set foot on Ottoman soil, he was betrayed by a fellow Greek to the Habsburg authorities, who promptly handed him and a small group of coconspirators over to the Ottoman authorities; he was subsequently strangled by them in Belgrade in the summer of 1798. At one level Rigas's conspiracy had thus been a miserable failure, but his almost single-handed crusade served as an inspiration to future generations of Greek nationalists.

WESTERN ENCROACHMENTS

The arrest of Rigas alarmed both the Ottoman authorities and the hierarchy of the Orthodox church, for it almost coincided with the occupation of the Ionian (Iónia) Islands in 1797 by the forces of revolutionary France and with Napoléon Bonaparte's invasion of Egypt in 1798. These developments caused panic in Constantinople, for they seemed to indicate that the seditious and atheistic doctrines of the French Revolution had penetrated the borders of the empire. The brief period of French rule in the Ionian Islands, which was attended by the rhetoric of revolutionary liberation, soon gave way to a short-lived Russo-Turkish condominium, a further period of French rule, and finally, after 1815, the establishment of a British protectorate. Although governed like a colony, the Ionian Islands under British rule, in theory, constituted an independent state and an example of free Greek soil, adjacent to but not under the control of the Ottoman Empire.

PHILIKÍ ETAIREÍA

The example of Rigas Velestinlis was very much in the minds of the three young Greeks, lowly members of the Greek mercantile diaspora, who in 1814 in Odessa (then in southern Russia, now in Ukraine), the centre of a thriving Greek community, founded the Philikí Etaireía, or "Friendly Society." Their specific aim was to lay the foundations for a coordinated, armed uprising against the Turks. The three founders—Emmanuil Xanthos, Nikolaos Skouphas, and Athanasios Tsakalov—had little vision of the shape of the independent Greece they sought beyond the liberation of the motherland.

The initiation rituals of the Philikí Etaireía were strongly influenced by those of the Freemasons. There were four categories of membership, ranging from the lowly *vlamis* (brother) to the *poimin* (shepherd). Those who betrayed the conspiracy were ruthlessly dispatched. Initially the society's attempt to recruit members throughout the Greek world met with little success, but from 1818 onward it made some headway, finding an important source of recruits in the communities of the diaspora. From the outset the leadership of the society—aware that the majority of the Greek people considered their fellow Orthodox believers, the Russians, to be their most likely liberators—misleadingly suggested that the conspiracy was backed by the Russian authorities.

Two attempts were made to recruit Count Ioánnis Kapodístrias—a Greek from Corfu (Kérkyra) who since 1816 had served as joint foreign minister to Tsar Alexander I of Russia and who was well versed in the ways of European diplomacy—as leader of the conspiracy. The conservative Kapodístrias, however, was dismissive of the plot and urged the Greeks to bide their time until there was another war between the Russian and Ottoman empires, when they might hope to achieve the kind of quasi-autonomy gained by Serbia in 1813. Although he could see no future in the plans of the members of the Philikí Etaireía, Kapodístrias did not betray the secret of the conspiracy. The leadership of the conspiracy was then transferred to another Greek in the Russian service, Prince Alexander Ypsilantis, a Phanariote who held the position of aide-de-camp to Alexander but who lacked the political experience of Kapodístrias.

Like Rigas Velestinlis, the conspirators were hoping for the support of the Romanians and the Bulgarians, but there was little enthusiasm for the project on the part of the other Balkan peoples, who were inclined to view the Greeks—with their privileged position in the Ottoman Empire and their enthusiasm for the ecclesiastical and cultural Hellenization of the other Balkan Christians—as scarcely less oppressive than the Turks.

Although unable to rely on the other Balkan peoples, the leadership of the conspiracy succeeded in exploiting the internal problems of the Ottoman Empire to its advantage. Sultan Mahmud II, who had ascended the throne in 1808, was bent on restoring the authority of the central government. In 1820, he launched an attack against Ali Paşa Tepelenë, a provincial warlord who, from his capital in Ioánnina, exercised control over large areas of mainland Greece. Although he nominally paid allegiance to the sultan, his virtual independence had for many years exasperated the Ottoman authorities. Taking advantage of the fact that large numbers of Ottoman troops were participating in the campaign against Ali Paşa, Alexander Ypsilantis launched an attack from Russian territory across the Pruth River in March 1821, invoking the glories of ancient Greece in his call to arms from Jassy (Iasi), the Moldavian capital. His campaign met little success, and he encountered no enthusiasm on the part of the supporters of Tudor Vladimirescu, who had risen against the oppression of the local Romanian boyars, or notables. Memories of Phanariote Greek oppression were altogether too vivid and recent. In June of 1821 Ypsilantis and his motley army were defeated at the battle of Drăgătsani, and Ypsilantis was forced dishonourably to flee into Habsburg territory, where he died in captivity in 1828.

REVOLT IN THE PELOPONNESE

Shortly after Ypsilantis's raid into Moldavia, scattered violent incidents coalesced into a major revolt in the Peloponnese. It is said to have begun on March 25, 1821—still celebrated as Greek

Independence Day—when Germanos, archbishop of Pátrai, unfurled a Greek flag at the monastery of Ayia Lavra near Kalávrita. With atrocities being committed by both sides, the Turks, very much in a minority, were forced to retreat to their coastal fortresses. The diversion of Ottoman forces for the attack on Ali Paşa, the element of surprise, and the military and especially naval skills on which the Greeks could draw gave the Greeks an advantage in the early years of what proved to be a lengthy struggle.

The revolt caught the public's attention in western Europe, even if in the early years the reactionary governments of post-Napoleonic Europe were not prepared to face any disturbance of the existing order. Public sympathy in western Europe was translated into more concrete expressions of support with the arrival in the Peloponnese of philhellene volunteers, the best-known of whom was the poet Lord Byron, who had traveled extensively in the Greek lands before 1821. The military contribution of the philhellenes was limited, and some became disillusioned when they discovered that Greek reality differed from the idealized vision of Periclean Athens in which they had been nurtured in their home countries. The philhellenic committees that sprang up in Europe and the United States, however, soon raised money for the prosecution of the war and the relief of its victims, such as the survivors of the great massacre on Chíos in 1822, immortalized by the French painter Eugène Delacroix.

FACTIONALISM IN THE EMERGING STATE

At a very early stage in the fighting, the question of the governance of the liberated territories came to light. Initially no fewer than three provisional governments coexisted, while in 1822 a constitution, which by the standards of the day was highly democratic, was adopted with the hope of securing the support of the people in Europe. A revised constitution was adopted in 1823, at which time the three local governments were unified in a central authority. However, unification did not bring unity. Feuding between rival groups culminated in outright civil war in 1824, prompting one chieftain, Makriyannis, to protest that he had not taken up arms against the Turks in order to end up fighting Greeks.

Such factionalism derived from a number of causes. There was a basic tension between the *kodjabashis*, or notables, of the Peloponnese, who were anxious to ensure that they retained the privileged status they had held under the Ottomans, and the military element, associated with such klephtic leaders as Theódoros Kolokotrónis, who sought recognition in terms of political power for their contribution to the war effort. The island shipowners, whose contribution to the prosecution of the war at sea was vital, likewise laid claim to a share of power, while the small intelligentsia argued for the adoption of liberal parliamentary institutions. To some degree the clash can be seen as a confrontation

THEÓDOROS KOLOKOTRÓNIS

As a member of the Greek revolutionary society Philikí Etaireía, Theódoros Kolokotrónis (born April 1770, Messenia [Greece]—died February 15, 1843, Athens) led Moreot bands during the War of Independence. His most brilliant action was his part in the defeat of Mahmud Dramali's Ottoman army in August 1822. He was imprisoned on Hydra for his defiance of the central government but was later released to help defend the Morea (Peloponnese) against the Egyptians. In 1825 he signed the Greek demand for British protection and invited Sir Richard Church to be Greek commander in chief. In 1828 he supported the president, Count I.A. Kapodístrias, and became one of the leaders of the pro-Russian party. After the count's assassination on October 9, 1831, Kolokotrónis set up a rival administration favouring 17-year-old Prince Otto of Bavaria for the newly created Greek throne, and he later tried to overthrow the young king's regency, composed largely of Bavarians. For this, Kolokotrónis was condemned to death on June 7, 1834, but was later reprieved.

between Westernizers and traditional elites and to some degree as a clash between the military and civilian parties. The Westernizers, who were nationalistic and whose attitudes were expressed by their adoption of a Western lifestyle, wanted independent Greece to develop along the lines of a European state, with a regular army and with a curb on the traditional powers of the church. The traditional elites, on the other hand, tended to see the struggle in terms of a religious crusade against the Muslims, and their national consciousness was less fully articulated. Anxious to maintain the power and privileges they had enjoyed before the struggle began, they were chiefly concerned with substituting the oligarchy of the Turks with one of their own.

The insurgents could not permit internecine fighting. Mahmud II had by this time forged an alliance with his nominal subject, Muḥammad ʿAlī, the ruler of Egypt, and his son Ibrahim Pasha, who were promised lavish territorial rewards in return for their assistance in suppressing the revolt. Beginning in early 1825, Ibrahim Pasha engaged in a bitter war with the insurgents. As their initially favourable military position deteriorated, the insurgents looked increasingly for salvation from the great powers (Russia, France, and Great Britain), which, from a combination of mutual suspicion as to each other's objectives and concern at the damage being done to their commercial interests, gradually moved toward a more interventionist position.

In 1826, by the Protocol of St. Petersburg, Britain and Russia committed themselves to a policy of mediation, to which France became a party through the Treaty of London of 1827. A policy of "peaceful interference," as the British prime minister Lord Canning described it, culminated in the somewhat planned destruction of the Turco-Egyptian fleet by a combined British, French, and Russian fleet at the Battle of Navarino in October 1827, the last great naval battle of the age of sail. This intervention by the great powers was instrumental in ensuring that some form of independent Greece came into existence, although its precise borders, which ran from Árta in the west to Vólos in the east, took some years to negotiate. This process was overseen by Count Ioánnis Kapodístrias, who was elected the first president of Greece by the Assembly of Troezene, which in 1827 enacted the third constitution of the independence period.

Besides overseeing the negotiation of the boundaries of the new state, in which his extensive diplomatic experience in the Russian imperial service was fully employed, Kapodístrias was also completely engaged in trying to establish the infrastructure of a state in a country that had been ravaged by a vicious and destructive war. Schooled

Painting depicting the Battle of Navarino, the decisive naval engagement of the Greek war of independence. Navarino was also the last major naval battle fought by wooden ships. SuperStock

in the traditions of Russian autocracy, Kapodístrias chafed under the provisions of the 1827 constitution, which, like its predecessors, was a remarkably liberal document, and he abolished it. His paternalist and authoritarian style of government offended a number of key elements in the hierarchy of the embryonic Greek state. Growing unrest culminated in his assassination in Nauplia (Návplio), the provisional capital, in October 1831.

BUILDING THE NATION, 1832–1913

Greece's existence as an independent state gained formal recognition in the treaty of 1832 between Bavaria and the great powers, but the Greeks themselves were not involved in the making of the treaty. Greece formally became a sovereign state, and the Greeks became the first of the subject peoples of the Ottoman Empire to gain full independence.

IOÁNNIS ANTÓNIOS, COUNT KAPODÍSTRIAS

Ioánnis Antónios, Count Kapodístrias (b. February 11, 1776, Corfu [Greece]—d. October 9, 1831 Návplion, Greece), was a Greek statesman who was prominent in the Russian foreign service during the reign of Alexander I (reigned 1801–25) and was a leader in the Greek struggle for independence.

The son of Count Antonio Capo d'Istria, he was born in Corfu (at that time under Venetian rule), studied at Padua, and then entered government service. In 1799 Russia and Turkey drove the French from the Ionian Islands and organized them into the Septinsular Republic. Kapodístrias participated in writing the new state's second constitution (adopted 1803) and became its secretary of state (1803). France regained control of the islands (1807), however, and Kapodístrias entered the Russian foreign service (1809). He became an expert on Balkan affairs, which earned him a post with the commander of Russia's armed forces on the lower Danube River (1812). After the army marched north to oppose Napoleon's invasion of Russia (1812), Kapodístrias was assigned as a diplomat to the army staff (1813) and later was sent by Alexander I on a special mission to Switzerland (1814).

After attending the postwar Congress of Vienna as one of Russia's representatives (1814–15), Kapodístrias became a highly influential adviser of the emperor; and, after January 1816, he was given equal responsibility with Karl Robert Nesselrode, the director of the Ministry of Foreign Affairs, for the conduct of Russia's foreign policy.

Kapodístrias, however, expressed doubts about Alexander's Holy Alliance with Austria and Prussia and objected to Russia's approval of Austria's suppression of the revolts in Naples and Piedmont (1820–21). Consequently, he earned the political enmity of Austria's chancellor Metternich, who used his increasing influence over Alexander to undermine Kapodístrias's position. When Alexander refused to support the Greek revolt against

Turkey (begun March 1821), Kapodístrias, who had a deep sympathy for the cause of Greek independence, although he had earlier refused to lead the major Greek revolutionary organization, found himself in an intolerable position. In 1822, therefore, he took an extended leave of absence from the Russian service and settled in Geneva, where he devoted himself to supplying material and moral relief to the Greek rebels until April 1827, when he was elected provisional president of Greece.

Resigning from the Russian service, he then toured Europe seeking financial and diplomatic support for the War of Greek Independence and arrived at Návplion (Nauplia), Greece's capital, in January 1828. He subsequently directed his energies toward negotiating with Great Britain, France, and Russia (which had all joined the war against the Turks) over the settlement of Greece's frontiers and the selection of its new monarch. He became leader of a party with pro-Russian sympathies. He also worked to organize an effective government apparatus and to subordinate powerful, semiautonomous local leaders to the authority of the new state. In the process, however, he acquired many enemies, two of whom, Konstantinos and Georgios Mavromikhalis of Maina, assassinated Kapodístrias as he entered a church.

However, the state contained within its borders less than one-third of the Greek population of the Middle East, and the struggle to expand the country's borders came to dominate the first century of independent statehood. In 1947, with the incorporation of the Dodecanese (Dodekánisa)—a group of islands off the southwestern coast of Turkey that were under Italian rule—Greece's present borders were established.

GREECE UNDER OTTO OF WITTELSBACH

The sovereignty of the small Greek state was not absolute, despite gaining independence from the Ottoman Empire, and the great powers, which retained certain ill-defined rights of intervention, determined that Greece should become a monarchy. The great powers chose Otto of Wittelsbach—the 17-year-old son of King Louis I (Ludwig) of Bavaria—as king of Greece. Because he was still a minor, the great powers determined that, until Otto came of age, the country was to be ruled by three Bavarian regents while the army was to be composed of Bavarians. The period of the "Bavarokratia," as the regency was termed, was not a happy one, for the regents showed little sensitivity for the mores of Otto's adopted countrymen and imported European models of government, law, and education without regard to local conditions. The legal and educational systems were thus heavily influenced by German and French models, as was the church settlement of 1833, which ended the traditional authority of the ecumenical patriarch and subjected ecclesiastical affairs to civil control.

Even after the formal ending of the regency in 1835, the Bavarian presence remained strong and was increasingly resented by those who had fought for

Otto of Wittelsbach, the son of Bavarian King Louis I who was installed as the first monarch of the newly independent Greek state in the early 19th century. Universal Images Group/Getty Images.

independence. Another source of frustration for some was Otto's failure to grant a constitution, as had been provided for in the negotiations preceding independence. Despite the absence of a constitution, however, political parties of some sort came into existence; the "British," "Russian," and "French" parties were associated with the diplomatic representatives of the great powers, and their main appeal was strong personalities rather than well-defined ideologies.

Toward the end of the decade of the 1830s, people became increasingly discontent with Otto's rule. There was no indication that he would concede a constitution; Bavarians were still influential; his marriage to Queen Amalia had not produced an heir; the king remained a Roman Catholic in an Orthodox country with a strong anti-Catholic tradition; and much of the country's revenues were being expended in servicing the loan granted on independence by the protecting powers (France, Russia, and Great Britain).

These various strands of discontent coalesced in the military coup of September 1843. Nearly bloodless, the coup was the first of many military interventions in Greece's political process. Otto was forced to grant a constitution (promulgated in 1844), which was a liberal document by the standards of the day, providing for virtually universal manhood suffrage (although women were barred from voting until as late as 1952). However, Otto, together with his crafty prime minister, Ioánnis Koléttis, was able to overturn the new constitution by establishing a kind of parliamentary dictatorship. The attempt to implant a liberal constitutional democracy onto an essentially premodern, traditional society that had evolved in quite a different fashion from those of western Europe gave rise to tensions both within the political system and in the relations between state and society, which have carried on into modern times. *Rouspheti* (the reciprocal dispensation of favours), patronage, manipulation, and, at times, outright force continued to characterize the politics of the postconstitutional period.

THE GREAT IDEA

It was during the debates that preceded the promulgation of the 1844 constitution that Koléttis first coined the expression the "Great Idea" (Greek: *Megáli Idéa*). This was a visionary nationalist aspiration that was to dominate foreign relations and, to a significant extent, to determine the domestic politics of the Greek state for much of the first century of its independent existence.

If the expression was new in 1844, the concept was deeply rooted in the Greek popular psyche, nurtured by the prophecies and oracles that had kept hopes of eventual emancipation from the Turkish yoke alive and real during the dark centuries of the Tourkokratia. The Great Idea envisaged the restoration of the Orthodox Christian Byzantine Empire, with its capital once again established in Constantinople, which would be achieved by incorporating within the bounds of a single state all the areas of Greek settlement in the Middle East. Besides the Greek populations settled over a wide area in the southern Balkan Peninsula, there were extensive Greek populations in the Ottoman capital, Constantinople (Istanbul), itself; along the shores of the Sea of Marmara; along the western coastal region of Asia Minor, particularly in the region of Smyrna (İzmir); in central Anatolia (ancient Cappadocia), where much of the Greek populace was Turkish-speaking but employed the Greek alphabet to write Turkish; and in the Pontus region of northeastern Asia Minor, whose geographic isolation had given rise to an obscure form of Greek that was not understood elsewhere in the Greek world.

The Great Idea, the liberation by the Greek state of the "unredeemed" Greeks of the Ottoman Empire, was to be achieved through a combination of military means—an ambitious objective for a state with such limited resources—and a far-reaching program of educational and cultural propaganda aimed at instilling a sense of Hellenic identity in the very large Greek populations that remained under Ottoman rule. The University of Athens (1837) attracted people from all parts of the Greek world to be trained as students and apostles of Hellenism.

Greece hoped to profit from the Crimean War (1854–56) fought between Russia—the only sovereign Orthodox power—and the Ottoman Empire and its British and French allies. However, Greek neutrality in the conflict was enforced by a British and French occupation of Piraeus, the port of Athens; this was just one of several interventions in Greece's internal affairs by the great powers that made light of Greece's sovereign status.

King Otto's enthusiasm for the Great Idea at the time of the Crimean War was popular with his subjects, but during the 1850s there was renewed discontent. The manipulation of the 1844 constitution had alienated a younger generation of politicians who had not been directly involved in the war of independence. Otto had also still not converted to the Orthodox church, nor had he an heir. The king was driven into exile following a coup in 1862 and spent the rest of his days in exile in Bavaria.

REFORM, EXPANSION, AND DEFEAT

The downfall of King Otto forced the great powers to search for a new sovereign who could not be drawn from their own dynasties. Their choice was a prince of the Danish Glücksburg family, who reigned as King George I of the Hellenes from 1863 to 1913; thereafter the Glücksburg dynasty reigned intermittently until the 1974 referendum rejected the institution of monarchy. To mark the beginning of the new reign, Britain ceded to Greece the Ionian Islands, over which it had exercised a protectorate since 1815—the first accession of territory to the Greek state since independence.

POLITICAL MODERNIZATION

A new constitution in 1864 amplified the democratic freedoms of the 1844 constitution, although the sovereign retained substantial, and somewhat vaguely defined, powers in foreign policy. However, the realities of politics remained much as before, with numerous elections and even more frequent changes of administration as politicians formed short-lived coalitions, jockeying for power in the disproportionately large parliament. In 1875 a decisive step was taken toward political modernization when King George acknowledged that he would entrust the government to the political leader that demonstrated the confidence of a majority of the deputies in parliament.

During the last quarter of the 19th century the kaleidoscopic coalitions of earlier years gave way to a two-party system in which power alternated between two men: Kharílaos Trikoúpis and Theódoros Dhiliyiánnis. Trikoúpis represented the modernizing, Westernizing trend in politics, and Dhiliyiánnis was a political boss in the traditional mold with no real program other than overturning the reforms of his archrival. Believing the modernization of the political system and economic development to be the essential preconditions of territorial expansion, Trikoúpis struggled to establish Greece's credit in international markets and encouraged the country to industrialize. He also promoted such infrastructural projects as road building, railway construction, the building of the Corinth Canal, and the draining of Lake Kopaïs in Thessaly. Such measures, however, in addition to Trikoúpis's parallel efforts to

GEORGE I

The long reign of George I (b. December 24, 1845, Copenhagen, Denmark—d. March 18, 1913, Thessaloníki, Greece) as king of Greece (1863–1913) spanned the formative period for the development of Greece as a modern European state. His descendants occupied the throne until the military coup d'état of 1967 and eventual restoration of the republic in 1973.

Born Prince William, the second son of King Christian IX of Denmark and the brother of Queen Alexandra of England, he was nominated to the Greek throne by Britain, France, and Russia after the first Greek king, Otto, was deposed in 1862. The National Assembly accepted William as king of the Hellenes in March 1863, and he ascended the throne as George (Georgios) I on October 31. Although the early years of his reign were dominated by his harsh and unpopular adviser Count Sponneck, who was obliged to return to Denmark in 1877, he refrained from transgressing the prerogatives of the National Assembly and became one of the most successful constitutional monarchs in Europe.

modernize the country's armed forces, required funding, and the increased taxation they entailed proved an easy target for a populist demagogue such as Dhiliyiánnis. Dhiliyiánnis became increasingly popular by advocating an aggressive policy toward the Ottoman Empire, but his belligerence was to have disastrous economic consequences.

EXTENSION OF GREEK BORDERS

If Britain had hoped to suppress irredentist enthusiasm by ceding the Ionian Islands, it was sorely mistaken. The continuing agitation on the "Great Island" of Crete for union with the Greek kingdom, which erupted in periodic uprisings, caused inevitable friction in relations with the Ottoman Empire. Greece also made a rather inept attempt to exploit the latter's discomfiture in the great Middle Eastern crisis of 1875–78, which gave rise to a war between Russia and the Ottoman Empire. The great powers, meeting in Berlin in 1878, in addition to cutting down the size of "Big Bulgaria," which had arisen from the conflict, pressed the Ottoman government to cede the rich agricultural province of Thessaly and a part of Epirus to Greece. In 1881 the second extension of the territory of the independent state came into being, like the first—the cession of the Ionian Islands—as a result of mediation by the great powers rather than of armed conflict. In 1878, again as part of the Berlin settlement, the island of Cyprus, with its largely Greek population, came under British administration but remained

formally under Ottoman sovereignty. The island was annexed by Britain in 1914, after the Ottoman Empire entered World War I on the side of the Central Powers, and became a crown colony in 1925.

RECTIFICATION OF FRONTIERS

The incorporation of Thessaly brought the northern frontier of Greece to the borders of Macedonia, which, with its mixed population of Greeks, Bulgarians, Serbs, Albanians, Turks, Vlachs, and Roma (Gypsies), was characterized by a great deal of ethnic complexity. It also brought Greece into contention with Serbia and Bulgaria, both of which also looked to Macedonia, which remained under Ottoman rule, with covetous eyes. The contest was initially conducted by means of ecclesiastical, educational, and cultural propaganda, but at the turn of the century rival guerrilla bands, financed by their respective governments (and supported by the public), sought to achieve by terror what they could not achieve by more peaceful means.

While Trikoúpis argued for the strengthening of the state as the basic precondition of territorial expansion, Deliyannis showed no such caution. His mobilization of forces in 1885 in an attempt to exploit a crisis over Bulgaria resulted in the establishment of a naval blockade by the great powers, while his support for the insurgents in Crete in 1897 led to a humiliating defeat in the Thirty Days' War with Turkey. Greece was forced to pay compensation and to accept the adjustments made to its frontier. Another humiliation sovereign Greece faced was the installation of an international financial commission to oversee the repayment of its substantial external debts.

EMIGRATION

Military endeavours compounded serious economic problems, which culminated in national bankruptcy in 1893. Economic difficulties were primarily responsible for the great wave of emigration, principally from the Peloponnese to the United States, that characterized the late 19th and early 20th centuries. About one-sixth of the entire population participated in this great exodus, the vast majority being male. The early emigrants had little intention of settling permanently overseas, though few ever returned to their homeland. Migrant remittances to relatives in the old country subsequently made a significant contribution to the country's balance of payments.

THE EARLY VENIZÉLOS YEARS

What the Greeks learned from the 1897 war was that, however weakened the Ottoman state might be, Greece was in no position to engage in single-handed military confrontation. Allies and the reinvigoration of the ill-constructed state and economy were the necessary prerequisites for a successful military threat. The latter came about under the inspired leadership of Eleuthérios Venizélos, who had emerged in the politics of his native Crete, where an autonomous regime had been established following the 1897 war. A charismatic figure who was adored and denounced in equal measure, Venizélos dominated Greek politics during the first three decades of the 20th century.

THE GOUDI COUP

Venizélos was projected from the provincial to the national stage as a consequence of a coup staged by the Military League, formed by disaffected army

MILITARY LEAGUE

The Military League (Greek: Stratiotikos Syndesmos) was a group of young Greek army officers who, emulating the Young Turk Committee of Union and Progress, sought to reform their country's national government and reorganize the army. The league was formed in May 1909 and was led by Colonel Nikolaós Zorbas. In August 1909 the Athens garrison moved to the neighbouring Goudhi Hill and forced the resignation of Premier Demetrios Rhalles, replacing him with Kyriakoules Mavromichales. It also forced King George I to dismiss his sons from military commands. The league found itself unable to create a new political system, however, and therefore summoned the Cretan politician Eleuthérios Venizélos to Athens (Modern Greek: Athína) as its political adviser. Venizélos persuaded the king to revise the constitution and asked the league to disband in favour of a National Assembly. In March 1910 the Military League dissolved itself.

officers, from Goudi (at the outskirts of Athens) in 1909. This coup ushered in a persistent pattern of military involvement in politics during the 20th century. The conspirators demanded thorough reforms of both a nonmilitary and a military nature, the latter including the removal of the royal princes, who often promoted their own protégés, from the armed forces.

VENIZÉLOS'S REFORMIST PROGRAM

The short-lived but forceful intervention of the military compelled the discredited political establishment to make way for Venizélos, who had not been compromised by involvement in the petty politics of the kingdom. In elections held in December 1910 Venizélos and his newly founded Liberal Party won more than four-fifths of the seats in parliament. His power legitimized through elections, Venizélos plunged into a wide-ranging program of constitutional reform, political modernization, and economic development, which he combined with an energetic enthusiasm for the Great Idea. Some 50 amendments to the 1864 constitution were enacted; provision was made for land reform; innovations were made in the educational system; and legislation benefiting the working population was introduced. However, these moderately reformist policies inhibited the development of the powerful agrarian and socialist movements that developed elsewhere in the Balkans. British naval and French military missions were brought in to overhaul the armed forces. Venizélos's continuing political ascendancy was confirmed with a sweeping victory in elections held in 1912.

THE BALKAN WARS

The defeat of 1897 had induced much pessimism but gave way to a period of optimism, in which Greece splendiferously saw itself as a rising power poised to displace a declining Ottoman Empire as the leading power in the Middle East. In 1911, when Italy attacked the Ottoman Empire—in the process occupying the largely Greek-populated Dodecanese—Greece, no less than the other Balkan states, wanted its share of the spoils from the ever more likely collapse of Ottoman rule in the Balkans. However, Greece's situation differed from that of its Balkan neighbours, whose populations were relatively and compactly settled within the Balkan Peninsula. The Greeks, on the other hand, were widely dispersed throughout the Middle East and thus vulnerable to Turkish reprisals in the event of a war. But Greece could scarcely stand aside from the network of alliances being formed among the Balkan states. These culminated in October 1912 in the First Balkan War, with Greece, Serbia, Bulgaria, and Montenegro declaring war on the Ottoman Empire. In contrast to earlier Balkan crises, the great powers did not intervene, and the heavily outnumbered Ottoman forces were forced into rapid retreat. Within less than a month, Thessaloníki (Salonika; Thessalonica), the most important port in the northern Aegean, coveted by Bulgaria as well as by Greece, was captured by Greek forces. In February 1913 Greek forces took Ioánnina, the capital of Epirus. Meanwhile the Greek navy rapidly occupied the Aegean islands still under Ottoman rule.

The Balkan alliance was always a somewhat fragile affair in view of rivalries over Macedonia. Bulgaria, in particular, felt that its sacrifices had been in vain and turned against its former allies Greece and Serbia. This brief Second Balkan War (June to July 1913) led to the Treaty of Bucharest (August 1913), in which Bulgaria was forced to acknowledge the acquisition by Greece and Serbia of a substantial proportion of Macedonia. At the same time the formal union of Crete with the kingdom was recognized, although Greek hopes for the annexation of northern Epirus, with its large Greek population, were thwarted when the region was incorporated into newly independent Albania.

The expansion of Greece's territories in the First and Second Balkan Wars was extensive. Its land area had increased by more than three-fifths, and so had its population (from about 2.8 million to 4.8 million), but by no means were all of its newly acquired citizens ethnic Greeks. In the city of Thessaloníki the largest single element in the city's population was made up of Sephardic Jews, the descendants of the Jews expelled from Spain in 1492, most of whom continued to speak Ladino. Elsewhere in "New Greece," as the recently acquired territories came to be known, there were substantial Slavic, Muslim (mainly Turkish), Vlach, and Roma populations. Like the Jews, many of these populations did not look upon the Greeks as liberators. The integration of "New" with "Old" Greece, the conservative core of the original kingdom, would not be an easy process, but the problems it created did not emerge until much later.

At the conclusion of hostilities and under the charismatic leadership of Venizélos, the irredentist aspirations enshrined in the Great Idea appeared to be within reach. When King George I died at the hands of a deranged assassin in March 1913, there were demands that his successor, Crown Prince Constantine, be crowned not Constantine I (as he was) but Constantine XII to symbolize continuity with Constantine XI Palaeologus, the last emperor of Byzantium.

CHAPTER 12

GREECE SINCE WORLD WAR I

The dynamism and sense of national unity that had characterized the early Venizélos years gave way to rancour and vengefulness that were to poison the country's political life throughout World War I and the interwar period. Greece was torn apart by the "National Schism," a division of the country into irreconcilable camps supporting either King Constantine I or his prime minister, Venizélos.

FROM THE NATIONAL SCHISM TO DICTATORSHIP

The immediate grounds for tension were differences between the king and the prime minister as to Greece's alignment during World War I, although there were deeper causes underlying the split. The king advocated neutrality, while Venizélos was an enthusiastic supporter of the Triple Entente—Britain, France, and Russia—which he regarded as the alliance most likely to favour the implementation of Greece's remaining irredentist ambitions. The entente had, in an effort to lure Greece into the war, held out the prospect of territorial gain for Greece at the expense of Turkey, which had aligned itself with the Central Powers. Increasingly bitter disagreements between king and prime minister resulted in the latter twice resigning in 1915, despite a convincing electoral victory.

The breach between the two became irrevocable when Venizélos in October 1916 established a rival government in Thessaloníki, which, like most of "New Greece," was

Greek prime minister Eleuthérios Venizélos and King Constantine I during the Balkan War. Tensions between the two men would eventually cause a political schism in Greece that lasted into the 1930s. Herbert Orth/Time & Life Pictures/Getty Images

passionately loyal to Venizélos. In June 1917 the entente allies ousted King Constantine and installed Venizélos as prime minister of a formally united but bitterly divided Greece. Venizélos duly brought Greece, which was up to that time neutral, into the war on the side of the entente. Naturally, he expected to reap the rewards for his loyalty at the Paris Peace Conference. In May of 1919 Greece was permitted to land troops in İzmir (Smyrna), the major port city in Asia Minor, with a large Greek population. Greece also was a major beneficiary of the Treaty of Sèvres of August 1920, the peace treaty with the defeated Ottoman Empire. However, for the Turkish nationalists, incited by the leadership of Mustafa Kemal (Atatürk), the treaty was from the outset a dead letter and the Greek landings a challenge they were prepared to meet.

In November 1920 Venizélos was somewhat surprisingly defeated in elections, and the exiled King Constantine I was restored to his throne after a fraudulent plebiscite —to the obvious displeasure of Britain and France. Meanwhile, the military situation in Asia Minor steadily deteriorated; a Turkish nationalist offensive in August–September 1922 resulted in a dramatic rout of the Greek armies in Asia Minor. Much of İzmir was burned, and many Greeks and Armenians were killed. Tens of thousands of destitute Greek refugees fled to the kingdom of Greece, thus ending a 2,500-year Greek presence in Asia Minor and with it the elusive vision of the Great Idea.

A military junta seized power in 1922 as King Constantine abdicated, and five royalist politicians and the commander of the Asia Minor forces were tried and executed on a charge of high treason, although there was no evidence of deliberate treachery. The "Trial of the Six" was to poison the climate of interwar politics, exacerbating the already bitter feud between the supporters of Venizélos and of the monarchy.

At a peace conference in Lausanne, Greece and the newly established Turkish Republic agreed on an exchange of populations between the two countries. Religion was the criterion for the project, which resulted in the exchange of thousands of Turkish-speaking Orthodox Christians for Greek-speaking Muslims. The ecumenical patriarchate was allowed to remain in Constantinople, as were the Greek inhabitants of that city and of two islands, Imbros (now Gökçe) and Tenedos (Turkish: Bozcaada), which straddled the entrance to the strategically sensitive Dardanelles. In return, the Muslims of Greek Thrace were allowed to remain.

An influx of some 1.3 million refugees—including significant numbers from Russia and Bulgaria—strongly tested the social fabric of a country exhausted by some 10 years of intermittent war. Leaving aside the prejudice that they encountered on the part of the indigenous population, the process of their integration into Greek society was remarkably successful. The economy, benefiting from the entrepreneurial skills of the refugees, underwent a significant degree of industrialization during the interwar period. The remaining large estates were broken up to provide smallholdings for the newcomers, and rural Greece became a society of peasant smallholders, which made for social stability rather than for economic efficiency.

The majority of the refugees were settled in the territories of "New Greece," thereby consolidating the area's "Greekness." Although refugees were disproportionately represented in the leadership of the newly founded Communist Party of Greece (KKE), they largely remained intensely loyal to Venizélos. Their vote was clearly instrumental in the formal establishment of a republic in 1923, shortly after the departure of King George II, who had briefly succeeded to the throne following his father's abdication in 1922. The refugees and the army acted as the arbiters of political life during the interwar period.

In 1928 Venizélos made a political comeback, two years after the downfall of the short-lived military dictatorship headed by Gen. Theodoros Pangalos in 1925–26. Although Venizélos initiated a good-neighbour policy with Italy and Greece's Balkan neighbours and brought about a remarkable rapprochement with Turkey, his government felt the repercussions of the Wall Street stock market crash of 1929. Because Greece was dependent on the export of agricultural products such as olive oil, tobacco, and currants and on migrant remittances, it was severely affected by the decline in world trade.

After four years of relative stability, politics reverted to the chaos of the early 1920s. When the anti-Venizélists won the 1933 elections, Col. Nikólaos Plastíras, a staunch supporter of Venizélos and the mastermind behind the 1922 coup, sought to restore Venizélos to power by force. His coup was unsuccessful and was subsequently followed by an assassination attempt on Venizélos. The political arena was once again split between supporters of Venizélos and of the monarchy. Fear of a royalist restoration lay behind another attempted coup by Venizélist officers in March 1935. His proven involvement on this occasion forced Venizélos into exile in France, where he died shortly afterward, but not before he urged his supporters to reconcile with the king.

The royalists were the main beneficiaries of the abortive 1935 coup, in the aftermath of which King George II had been restored to his throne, following another dubious plebiscite. Like Venizélos in exile, the king on his return to Greece was in a conciliatory mood. However, elections held under a system of proportional representation in January 1936 produced a deadlock between the two main parliamentary blocs, the Venizélists and the royalists. Both blocs engaged in secret negotiations with the communists, who up to that time had been an insignificant force, but now, with 15 seats in the 300-seat parliament, held the balance of power.

THE METAXAS REGIME AND WORLD WAR II

Public disillusionment with the endless political corruption, which had been growing swiftly in the preceding years, was exacerbated when the news broke that the main political blocs were secretly negotiating with the communists. When the nonpolitical figure who headed a caretaker government charged with overseeing the elections died, he was replaced as prime minister by Gen. Ioannis Metaxas, a right-wing and lesser-known figure. Metaxas exploited labour unrest and a threatened general strike to persuade the king in August 1936 to suspend key articles of the constitution. Although the suspension was intended to be temporary, parliament did not reconvene for another decade.

Backed by the army and tolerated by the king, the Metaxas dictatorship lasted more than four years. The dictator —whose paternalistic style was signaled by the adoption of such titles as "National Father," "First Peasant," and "First Worker"—shared a dislike for parliamentary democracy, liberalism, and communism that was characteristic of German Nazism and Italian Fascism, but the "Regime of the Fourth of August

1936" simply lacked their dynamism. The government led by Metaxas did not seek alliances with the European dictatorships. On the contrary, with the support of the king, Metaxas strove to maintain the country's traditional alignment toward Britain. The dictator, however, endeavoured to recast the Greek character in a more disciplined mode, invoking the values of ancient Greece and, in particular, of the Spartans. He also sought to fuse them with the values of the medieval Christian empire of Byzantium, thus fashioning what he pompously described as the "Third Hellenic Civilization."

At the outbreak of World War II, Metaxas tried to maintain neutrality, but Greece was increasingly subject to pressure from Italy, whose dictator Benito Mussolini sought an easy military triumph to match those of his ally Adolf Hitler. A series of provocations culminated in the delivery of a humiliating ultimatum on October 28, 1940. Metaxas, reflecting the mood of the entire country, rejected this with a simple answer: "No!" The Italians immediately invaded Greece from Albania, which they had occupied 18 months previously. Any hopes of a lightning military triumph were quickly lost. Within weeks not only had the Italians been driven from Greek territory, but Greek forces had pushed on to occupy much of what the Greeks term "Northern Epirus," the area of southern Albania with a substantial Greek minority.

Though he accepted token British military aid, Metaxas, until his death in January 1941, was anxious to avoid provoking German intervention in the conflict. However, his successor agreed to accept a British expeditionary force as it became apparent that Hitler's aggressive designs extended to the Balkans. The combined Greek and British forces, however, were able to offer only limited resistance when the Germans crossed the borders in April 1941. British and Commonwealth troops were forced to retreat from superior German forces but managed to get to Crete, where they held out for 10 days against German parachute and glider troops. By the beginning of June the country was overrun and subjected to a harsh tripartite German, Italian, and Bulgarian occupation. King George II and his government-in-exile fled to the Middle East. The requisitioning of food stocks resulted in a terrible famine during the winter of 1941–42, in which as many as 100,000 people died. In 1943 virtually the entire Jewish population was deported to German death camps —most to Auschwitz. A devastatingly high rate of inflation added to the miseries and humiliations of everyday life.

Almost from the outset of the occupation, acts of resistance were recorded. These took a more systematic form after the Communist Party in September 1941 founded the National Liberation Front (Ethnikón Apeleftherotikón Métopon; EAM), whose military arm was known

EAM-ELAS AND EDES

EAM-ELAS (Greek: Ethnikón Apeleftherotikón Métopon–Ethnikós Laïkós Apeleftherotikós Strátos, English: National Liberation Front–National Popular Liberation Army) was a communist-sponsored resistance organization (formed September 1941) with a military wing (formed December 1942), which operated in occupied Greece during World War II. Fighting against the Germans and the Italians as well as against other guerrilla bands, particularly EDES, EAM-ELAS became the most powerful guerrilla band in the country. It also established an effective administrative apparatus, through which it ruled liberated areas.

By October 1944, when the Germans evacuated Greece, EAM controlled about two-thirds of the country. It participated in conferences in September 1944 that were designed to unite the rival resistance groups and the government-in-exile in a postwar government. When the new government ordered ELAS to disarm, however, the resistance group refused, causing an outbreak of hostilities in Athens in December 1944, mainly between ELAS and the British. A peace treaty was signed (Varkiza Peace Agreement, February 12, 1945), providing for the surrender of ELAS. A large-scale guerrilla war was begun by the communists in 1946, however, and lasted until 1949.

EDES (Greek: Ellínikos Dímokratikos Ethnikós Strátos; English: Greek Democratic National Army) was a nationalist guerrilla force that, bolstered by British support, constituted the only serious challenge to EAM-ELAS's control of the resistance movement in occupied Greece during World War II. Led by Gen. Napoleon Zervas, EDES was originally liberal and antimonarchist, but it moved steadily to the political right. It cooperated with ELAS for a time in operations against the Germans and Italians, but, between October 1943 and February 1944, the two guerrilla groups fought each other. The British hoped to build EDES into a force strong enough to rival EAM-ELAS, but it was incapable of extending its influence far beyond Epirus. During the fighting between ELAS and the British, which began in December 1944, the EDES army was destroyed by ELAS in four days.

as the Ellinikós Laikos Apeleftherotikós Strátos (ELAS). Although the communists had been a marginal force during the interwar period, EAM-ELAS became the largest resistance organization. Other groups came into being, the most important of which, the Greek Democratic Army (Ellinikós Dímokratikos Ethnikós Strátos; EDES), opposed—as did EAM-ELAS—the return of the king upon liberation. With the support of a British military mission, the guerrillas engaged in some spectacular acts of resistance, most notably the destruction in November 1942 of the Gorgopotamos viaduct, which carried the railway line from Thessaloníki to Athens, and in April 1944 the kidnapping and removal to Egypt of the German commander on Crete.

During this time of grave national crisis, just as during the war of independence and World War I, conflicts within groups divided the resistance organizations. Besides fighting the Axis occupation, they jockeyed for postwar power. During the winter of 1943–44, civil war broke out in the mountains of Greece between EAM-ELAS and the much smaller British-backed EDES, which had become increasingly alarmed at the prospect of a postliberation seizure of power by the communists.

Not for the first time in Greek history, the country's fate was to be determined by the great powers. The British prime minister, Winston Churchill, eager to restore King George II to his throne, engaged in the summer and autumn of 1944 in some high-level negotiations with the Soviet leader, Joseph Stalin, trading Russian predominance in postwar Romania for British predominance in Greece. It would seem that Stalin gave no encouragement to the Greek communists to make a bid for power in the autumn of 1944 as the Germans began their withdrawal, but by this time they were by far the most powerful force in occupied Greece.

The confrontation was only postponed, however, for bloody fighting broke out in Athens in December 1944 between EAM-ELAS and the small British force that had accompanied the Greek government on its return from exile in October. It was a sign of Churchill's obsession with the crisis in Greece that he flew to Athens on Christmas Eve 1944 in an unsuccessful attempt to resolve the conflict. The British prime minister, however, was able to persuade King George II not to return to Greece pending a plebiscite on the monarchy and to accept the regency of Archbishop Damaskinos of Athens. A temporary respite in the struggle between left and right was achieved at the Varkiza conference in February 1945, which aimed at a political settlement of the crisis.

CIVIL WAR AND ITS LEGACY

The first elections since the fateful ones of 1936 were held in March 1946. These were flawed and, with the far left abstaining, resulted in a sweeping victory for the royalist right. In September a plebiscite issued a vote for the return of King George II; he died within six months and his brother Paul succeeded him. Against this background the country slid toward civil war, as the far left was undecided as to whether to work within the political system or to make an armed bid for power.

The turning point came with the establishment in October 1946 of a communist-controlled Democratic Army, and the following year the communists established a Provisional Democratic Government. Although heavily outnumbered, the communists were able—with the logistical support from the newly established communist regimes to the north, coupled with skillful use of guerrilla tactics—to control a wide area of northern Greece for a substantial period of time. Following the declaration of the Truman Doctrine in March 1947, which pledged support for "free peoples" in their fight against internal subversion, the tide gradually began to turn. The United States, assuming Britain's former mantle as Greece's chief external patron, soon provided military equipment and advice. American intervention and the consequences of the break between Josip Broz Tito (under whose leadership the Yugoslav state would eventually unite) and Stalin, combined with factionalism

GEORGIOS PAPANDREOU

A Greek liberal politician who served three terms as prime minister, Georgios Papandreou (b. February 13, 1888, Kaléntzi, Greece—d. November 1, 1968, Athens) established a political dynasty that spanned three generations.

Papandreou studied at the University of Athens (L.L.D., 1911) and in Germany. He began his political career in 1915, served as governor of the Aegean Islands (1917–20), and was minister of education (1929–33) in the liberal antimonarchist government of Eleuthérios Venizélos. He broke away from the left wing of the Liberal Party and in 1935 founded the Democratic Socialist Party. During the dictatorship of Ioannis Metaxas, he was in exile, and he was imprisoned by the Germans in 1942–44 during World War II. Managing to escape, he then headed the Greek coalition government (initially a government-in-exile) from April 1944 until after the German army withdrew from Greece in October 1944, but he resigned in December of that year as the country slipped into civil war. From 1946 to 1952 he held ministerial posts in several governments. During a subsequent period in opposition, he merged his Democratic Socialist Party with the Liberal Party and in 1961 organized a new centre-left coalition, the Centre Union.

In 1963 the Centre Union won a bare electoral majority, and Papandreou became prime minister; but he resigned shortly afterward to seek an absolute majority, which he obtained in new elections in 1964. As prime minister Papandreou introduced a program of social reforms more far-reaching than those sought by previous governments, and he also criticized what he viewed as the excessive influence of the United States in his country. A crisis developed in 1965 over Papandreou's insistence on giving ministerial posts to his son Andreas, and he also clashed with the Greek king, Constantine, over the control of conservative officers in the army. In July 1965 the king dismissed Papandreou from the prime ministry, after which a period of political instability ensued in Greece. In 1967, when it became clear that Papandreou's party was again headed for victory in upcoming general elections, a military junta seized power in Greece and arrested Papandreou and his son Andreas. They were later released, but the elder Papandreou died soon afterward. Andreas went on to serve as prime minister (1981–1989; 1993–1996), and Georgios's grandson and namesake, George A. Papandreou, was elected prime minister in 2009.

and altered military tactics on the left, all contributed to the defeat of the communist guerrillas in the summer of 1949.

Greece emerged from the laborious 1940s in a state of devastation. The post-civil-war political regime was distinctly authoritarian, and from the mid-1950s Greece underwent a rapid but unevenly distributed process of economic and social development, far surpassing its communist neighbours to the north in standard of living. The population of greater Athens more than doubled in size between 1951 and 1981, and by the early 1990s about one-third of the entire population was concentrated in the area of the capital. However, if urbanization progressed quickly and living standards rose rapidly, the country's political institutions failed to keep pace with rapid change. The right maintained a firm grip on power for the majority of the period from 1952 to 1963 and was none too careful in the means it employed to retain it.

By the early 1960s, however, the electorate—which now included women—had become increasingly disillusioned with the repressive legacy of the civil war and sought change. Georgios Papandreou, whose Centre Union Party secured a sweeping victory in 1964, responded to this need as prime minister; yet the promise of reform and modernization was cast aside with renewed crisis in Cyprus, and groups within the army conspired to subvert the country's democratic institutions. A

guerrilla campaign in Cyprus—fought from the mid-1950s onward with tenacity and ruthlessness by the Greek-Cypriot general Georgios Grivas—had resulted in 1960 in the British conceding not the union with the Greek state sought by the overwhelming Greek-Cypriot majority on the island but rather independence. However, within three years the elaborate power-sharing arrangements between the Greek majority and the Turkish minority on the island had collapsed.

During and following the civil war, Greece's armed forces had come to look upon themselves not only as the country's guardians against foreign aggression but also as its defenders against internal subversion. They increasingly viewed Georgios Papandreou as a stalking horse for his much more radical American-educated son, Andreas Papandreou, who had returned to Greece and joined his father's government.

In April 1967, middle-ranking officers led by Col. Georgios Papadopoulos launched a coup designed to thwart an expected Centre Union victory in elections planned for May of that year. The conspirators took advantage of a prolonged political crisis, which had its origins in a dispute between the young King Constantine II, who had succeeded his father, King Paul, to the throne in 1964, and his prime minister, Georgios Papandreou. Alternating between policies that were heavy-handed and absurd, the "Colonels," as the military junta came to be known, misruled the country from 1967 to 1974. After a failed countercoup in December 1967, King Constantine went into exile, with Papadopoulos assuming the role of regent. In 1973 the monarchy was abolished, and Greece was declared a republic. That year, following student protests, which were violently suppressed, Papadopoulos himself was overthrown from within the junta and replaced by the even more repressive Gen. Demetrios Ioannidis, the head of the much-feared military police.

In July 1974, in the wake of an increasingly bitter dispute between Greece and Turkey over oil rights in the Aegean Sea, Ioannidis, seeking a nationalist triumph, launched a coup to depose Makarios III, the archbishop and president of Cyprus since 1960. Makarios survived, but the coup triggered the invasion of the northern part of the island by Turkey, which, together with Britain and Greece, was a guarantor of the 1960 constitutional settlement. The Turkish army occupied nearly two-fifths of the land area of the island, despite the fact that the Turkish population constituted less than one-fifth of the total population. Ioannidis responded to the Turkish invasion by mobilizing for war with Turkey. The mobilization proved chaotic, however, and the regime, bitterly unpopular domestically and totally isolated diplomatically, collapsed.

RESTORATION OF DEMOCRACY

Konstantinos Karamanlis, a conservative politician who had served as prime minister from 1955 to 1963, was summoned back from self-imposed exile in France to restore democracy and rebuild a country ravaged by seven years of brutal and inefficient military rule. The turnaround he accomplished was remarkable. He defused the threat of outright war with Turkey and ensured that the Greek army returned to the barracks. He acknowledged the way in which opposition to the junta had brought together politicians of all political backgrounds by legalizing the Communist Party, which had been outlawed in 1947. He moved rapidly to legitimize his power through elections held in November 1974, in which he secured a sweeping victory. In December a referendum on the future of the monarchy resulted in a majority vote against the monarchy and against the return of King Constantine.

Karamanlis's second premiership lasted from 1974 to 1980, when he was elected president. By this time he had achieved his main objective, early membership in the European Economic Community (later succeeded by the European Union [EU]), which Greece joined in January 1981. His failure to counter the populist appeal of Andreas Papandreou's Panhellenic Socialist Movement (PASOK), however, resulted in a stunning parliamentary electoral victory for PASOK in 1981.

The smooth transfer of power from a right-wing government that had ruled for much of the postwar period to a radical (at the level of rhetoric, at least) socialist government appeared to indicate that Greece's newly reestablished democratic institutions were firmly in place. Nevertheless, during almost a decade as prime minister, Papandreou failed to deliver on his promises of change, and a dramatic reorientation in the country's domestic politics and external relations never came about. Ambitious plans to "socialize" key sections of industry failed to materialize, and the attempt to create a welfare state could be sustained only by enormous borrowing. Important reforms were, however, introduced in family law, and society was liberalized in other respects. It was testimony to Papandreou's ability to articulate both the aspirations and the frustrations of a large segment of the electorate that, despite a poor economic record and amid accusations of large-scale corruption in the higher reaches of the party, the conservative New Democracy party (ND) barely regained power in 1990. The new government, with Konstantinos Mitsotakis as prime minister, was committed to a policy of economic liberalism and the diminution of the powers of the state, but the problems that confronted it were formidable. The rigid economic policies introduced by Mitsotakis and, in particular, proposals for the privatization of the large state sector, were unpopular with much of the electorate. In 1993 Papandreou's PASOK returned to power with a share of the vote only marginally smaller than it had received at the time of its electoral triumph in 1981.

However, the underlying economic and infrastructural problems facing Greece remained, and Papandreou was unable to do much to stop the rising deficits, inflation, interest rates, and unemployment as attempts to put Greece's finances on a sounder footing conflicted with PASOK's promises of social reforms. With Papandreou now in his mid-70s and in failing health, there were also disagreements within PASOK on who should become his successor. By January 1996, Papandreou was so incapacitated that he resigned; he died later that year. Konstantinos (Kostas) Simitis was elected as the new prime minister by the PASOK parliamentary deputies.

Simitis, more a pragmatic reformist than an ideological socialist, tried to control state spending and even to privatize some state industries. Hoping to capitalize on his apparent popularity, he called for elections in September, barely defeating the ND. In the late 1990s, Simitis's efforts to introduce some fundamental restructuring of Greece's economy brought some successes but also resistance from many Greeks. Much of the impetus for reforming Greece's economy came from its membership in the EU, though Greece struggled to meet the conditions needed to adopt in January

Rescuers, including emergency workers from Greek adversary Turkey, assist citizens in the aftermath of September 1999 earthquake that caused great destruction throughout the Greek capital of Athens. © AP Images

1999 the euro, the common currency of the EU.

In its foreign relations too, Greece continued to be preoccupied with disputes that upset other EU members. For years Greece refused to recognize the existence of the Republic of Macedonia, which had emerged as an independent country in 1991 after the breakup of the former Yugoslavia. Then Greece, after imposing a devastating economic embargo against Macedonia, reluctantly agreed in September 1995 to accept its existence under the name of the Former Yugoslav Republic of Macedonia. Greece has prevented Macedonia from becoming a member of NATO and of the EU, insisting that Greece has exclusive rights to the use of the name "Macedonia." Albanians, both in their homeland and in Greece, continued to be a source of irritation to Greeks, and, when NATO conducted its bombing campaign against Serbia in the spring of 1999 in support of the Albanian Kosovars, Greece refused to participate in the air attacks.

Earthquakes that devastated Turkey and Greece in the summer of 1999 led each country to provide rescue teams to aid the other, helping to thaw somewhat the centuries-old "cold war" between the two countries. And relations between them remained relatively stable, with solutions sought for problems related to Cyprus as that divided island prepared to join the EU. Tensions between the countries heated up again, however, in 2004 when Greek Cypriots voted against a UN-sponsored referendum on unification, and again in 2006, when a Greek and a Turkish plane collided, highlighting the countries' long-standing dispute over airspace.

Greece's economy maintained slow but steady growth throughout the early years of the 21st century, while the country prepared for Athens to host the 2004 Olympic Games. Despite construction delays, the needed infrastructure was in place on time, and the Games were a success that burnished Greece's international standing as a country with both a rich heritage and a promising future. The decade-long rule of PASOK came to a close in 2004 when Simitis's successor, Georgios Papandreou, son of Andreas Papandreou, lost to an ND led by Kostas Karamanlis (the nephew of Konstantinos Karamanlis), who was installed as prime minister. The economic reforms he introduced brought protests from some who dismissed them as neoliberal, but Karamanlis and his party retained control of the government in elections in 2007. The political mix remained volatile, and in December 2008 the killing of a teenage boy by a police officer in Athens set off weeks of rioting in the capital and other cities, primarily by angry, disaffected youth.

GREECE'S DEBT CRISIS

The Greek economy, like those of so many other countries, entered a period of uncertainty as a result of the international economic crisis of 2009, and the ND's hold on government appeared tenuous. In an attempt to reinforce his government's efforts to right the economy and seeking to shore up his position within his own party, Karamanlis called for snap elections in October 2009. The ND was swept from office in dramatic fashion, with a resurgent PASOK claiming 160 parliamentary seats—more than enough for an absolute majority. Karamanlis resigned as leader of the ND, and George Papandreou became the third member of his family to hold the post of prime minister.

In the wake of the election, it became clear that Greece's economic troubles were far worse than previously imagined. The borrowing by the ND government even before the international financial crisis, masked by misleading accounting, was revealed to have been excessive, and, with the onset of the broader economic meltdown, the Greek economy crumbled. Estimates of the Greek government's budget deficit put it at several times greater than that allowed by the rules governing the euro zone (countries whose currency is the euro). The reactive broad austerity measures that were introduced by the Papandreou government met with widespread protest and wildcat strikes domestically and were neither enough to provide for the government's short-term budget needs nor enough to stem the international financial market's concern with the impact of the Greek crisis on the value and stability of the euro. In March and April 2010 the EU and the International Monetary Fund (IMF) came to the rescue with two massive loan packages for Greece.

Even with the EU-IMF rescue, the Greek economy continued to struggle mightily. Growing dissatisfaction with the draconian budget cuts, reductions in benefits and pensions, and tax increases, as well as with Papandreou's handling of the crisis in general, led to more strikes and demonstrations in Athens, Thessaloníki, and elsewhere in the country. In June 2011 weeks of mass demonstrations outside the Greek parliament building—by protesters labeled the "indignants" (associated with similarly disenchanted Spaniards who had taken to the streets in response to the Spanish government's handling of its own debt crisis)—culminated in an eruption of violence. After failing in his attempts to form a government of "national unity," Papandreou reshuffled his cabinet, most notably appointing a new finance minister. All these events came as the EU and IMF contemplated delivery of the latest installment of the bailout, which was contingent on Greek implementation of ever-greater austerity measures along with the partial privatization of some state-owned companies. On June 21— facing the looming threat of default and all the ramifications it would entail for Greece and the euro zone—Papandreou's government narrowly survived a vote of confidence that set the stage for parliament to pass the necessary austerity measures on June 29 (contingent upon enactment the next day of new laws to facilitate the specific measures). Again the legislation was greeted with angry protests outside the parliament building, where demonstrators clashed with police.

EU leaders concluded an agreement on July 21 that extended more than €100 billion ($140 billion) in loans to Greece in an effort to stabilize the Greek economy and contain the potential damage to the euro zone as a whole. Interest rates for existing bailout loans were reduced, and the repayment periods were drastically lengthened. These changes came at a cost to private bondholders, however, and ratings agencies classified the restructuring as a "restricted default." This marked the first government debt default by a euro zone country since the implementation of the single currency.

At the end of October euro-zone leaders summited in Brussels in an attempt to hammer out a lasting solution for both the Greek and the broader European debt crisis. German Pres. Angela Merkel and French Pres. Nicolas Sarkozy met privately with Greece's creditors and engineered a bond swap that effectively cut the value of Greek debt in half. Only days after the plan was agreed upon, a firestorm of controversy erupted on October 31 when Papandreou announced his intention to submit the latest bailout plan to Greek voters in a referendum. Other European leaders, fearful that a no vote would render all their efforts moot and lead to dire consequences for the whole euro zone, were furious, and Papandreou's actions and motives were questioned not just by the Greek opposition but by many within his own party. As accusations and recriminations flew, Papandreou canceled the referendum after being assured of support for the bailout plan by ND leader Antonis Samaras, who nevertheless demanded Papandreou's resignation. Seemingly attempting to cling to power, Papandreou submitted to a vote of confidence on November 4, which he won by a small margin. He then agreed to step down as prime minister to pave the way for the formation of a "unity" government to facilitate approval of the most recent bailout plan. On November 11 Lucas Papademos—an adviser to Papandreou, and former vice president of the European Central Bank (ECB), who had overseen Greece's adoption of the euro as the governor of the Bank of Greece—became interim prime minister at the head of a coalition government. An economist, Papademos was widely seen as someone who would approach the challenge as a technocrat.

In February 2012 the Greek parliament approved more spending cuts that opened the door to an additional €130 billion (about $173 billion) in bailout funds from the ECB, the EU, and the IMF. Violent clashes between police and demonstrators erupted in Athens in April in response to the death near Greece's parliament of a man who committed suicide as an act of protest against deepening pension cuts. The widespread disenchantment among Greeks at the government's austerity measures was reflected in the results of parliamentary elections in May, which dealt a major blow to the country's long-time ruling parties. The ND finished first but garnered only about 19 percent of the vote. PASOK managed to get only some 13 percent of the vote, finishing third, behind the Syriza (Coalition of the Radical Left), which captured about 17 percent of the vote and was just one of a number of smaller antiausterity parties who were the real winners in the election, including the ultraright-wing nationalist Golden Dawn party, which registered about 7 percent of the vote. As the winner, the ND had the first opportunity to try to form a coalition government but was unable to do so, as were Syriza and PASOK, forcing a new election on June 17. This time the ND had a stronger showing, though again it only narrowly defeated Syriza, capturing about 30 percent of the vote to roughly 27 percent for Syriza and 12 percent for PASOK. Mindful that a minority of Greeks had voted for pro-bailout parties but still committed to the bailout (though hopeful that some of its terms might be renegotiated), ND leader Antonis Samaras took office as prime minister at the head of a coalition government that included PASOK and the smaller Democratic Left party.

CHAPTER 13

MALTA: THE LAND AND ITS PEOPLE

The island country of Malta is located in the central Mediterranean Sea. A small but strategically important group of islands, the archipelago has through its long and turbulent history played a vital role in the struggles of a succession of powers for domination of the Mediterranean and in the interplay between emerging Europe and the older cultures of Africa and the Middle East. As a result, Maltese society has been molded by centuries of foreign rule by various powers, including the Phoenicians, Romans, Greeks, Arabs, Normans, Sicilians, Swabians, Aragonese, Hospitallers, French, and British.

The island of Malta specifically played a vital strategic role in World War II as a base for the Allied Powers. It was

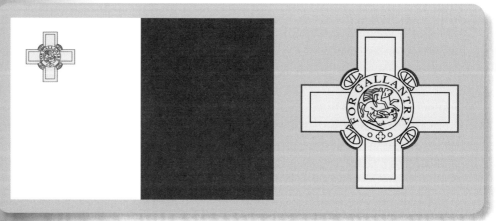

The flag of Malta. Encyclopaedia Britannica, Inc.

The coast of Malta features many bays and ports. Financial Times, London/Robert Harding Picture Library

heavily bombarded by German and Italian aircraft, and by the end of the war Malta was devastated. In 1942 the island of Malta was presented with the George Cross, a British award for great gallantry, in recognition of the wartime bravery of the Maltese people. After the war, the movement for self-governance became stronger. The country of Malta became independent from Britain and joined the Commonwealth in 1964 and was declared a republic on December 13, 1974. It was admitted to the European Union (EU) in 2004. A European atmosphere predominates in Malta as a result of close association with the Continent, particularly with southern Europe. The Maltese are renowned for their warmth, hospitality, and generosity to strangers, a trait that was noted in the Acts of the Apostles, with respect to the experience of St. Paul, the Apostle, who was said to have been shipwrecked off Malta in 60 CE.

Roman Catholicism is a major influence on Maltese culture. Various traditions have evolved around religious celebrations, notably those honouring

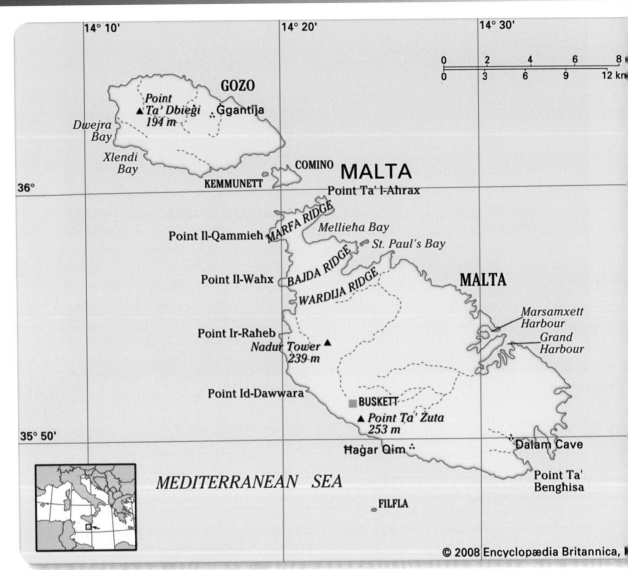

Map showing the islands of Malta.

the patron saints of towns and villages. The eight-pointed, or Maltese, cross, adopted by the Hospitallers of St. John of Jerusalem in 1126, is commonly linked with Malta's identity and is printed on the country's euro coin. Valletta is the capital city.

The country comprises five islands—Malta (the largest), Gozo, Comino, and the uninhabited islets of Kemmunett

(Comminotto) and Filfla—lying some 58 miles (93 km) south of Sicily, 180 miles (290 km) north of Libya, and about 180 miles (290 km) east of Tunisia, at the eastern end of the constricted portion of the Mediterranean Sea separating Italy from the African coast.

RELIEF

The islands of Malta are dominated by limestone formations, and much of their coastlines consist of steep or vertical limestone cliffs indented by bays, inlets, and coves. They lie on the submerged Malta-Hyblean Platform, a wide undersea shelf bridge that connects the Ragusa Platform of southern Sicily with the Tripolitana Platform of southern Libya.

The main physical characteristic of the island of Malta is a well-defined escarpment that bisects it along the Victoria Lines Fault running along the whole breadth of the island from Point ir-Raħeb near Fomm ir-Riħ Bay to the coast northeast of Għargħur at Madliena Fort. The highest areas are coralline limestone uplands that constitute a triangular plateau; Ta' Żuta, which rises to 830 feet (253 metres) in the southwest, is the highest point. The uplands are separated from the surrounding areas by blue clay slopes, while an undercliff area is found where the coralline plateau has fallen and forms a subordinate surface between

the sea and the original shore. The total shoreline of Malta is about 136 miles (219 km).

In northern Malta the escarpment is occasionally abrupt and broken by deep embayments. To the south, however, the plateau gradually descends from about 600 to 830 feet (180 to 250 metres) into undulating areas of globigerina (derived from marine protozoa) limestone less than 300 feet (90 metres) in elevation. The western area is characterized by deeply incised valleys and undercliff areas, while to the east there are several valley systems that descend to the central plains.

The west coast of Malta presents a high, bold, and generally harbourless face. On the east, however, a tongue of high ground known as Mount Sceberras, on which the capital city, Valletta, is built, separates Marsamxett Harbour and Grand Harbour. Because of tectonic activity, Malta has been tilted in a northerly direction, producing cliffs of up to about 800 feet (250 metres) high on the south and southwestern coasts, while slopes descend to low cliffs and rocky shores on the northern and eastern coasts.

The landscape of the island of Gozo is characterized by broken upper coralline mesas, with the highest point being Ta' Dbiegi Hill (636 feet [194 metres]). Gozo has a gentle easterly dip, so the lower coralline limestone, which forms high cliffs on the west

GOZO

Gozo (Maltese: Ghawdex), the second largest of the Maltese islands (after the island of Malta), is situated 3.25 miles (5.25 km) northwest of the nearest point of Malta. It is 9 miles long and 4.5 miles wide and has an area of 26 square miles (67 square km). It is also known as the "Island of the Three Hills," but in fact, the island has numerous conical knolls, which resemble extinct volcanoes. Gozo is not only hillier but also greener than the island of Malta. Its principal town, Victoria, also called Rabat, stands near the middle of the island on one of a cluster of steep hills in an intensively cultivated area. The megalithic temple Ggantija, to the east of Victoria, is noteworthy. Considered to be more fertile than Malta, Gozo depends heavily on agriculture, producing fruit, vegetables, grapes, and dairy products. Fishing is also important, and there is a cottage lace industry, but tourism is fast becoming the most important economic activity. The island is linked with Malta by ferry and helicopter service. Gozo is held to be the island of Ogy'gia, in Greek legend, where the sea nymph Calypso entertained Odysseus.

coast, declines to below sea level but reappears on the east coast at Qala Point. Semicircular bays have formed on coastal cliffs where sinkholes have been invaded by the sea. The rounded bays at Xlendi and Dwejra on the west coast of Gozo originated as underground caverns with roofs that have collapsed.

DRAINAGE

The island of Malta possesses favourable conditions for the percolation and underground storage of water. The impermeable blue clays provide two distinct water tables between the limestone formations—the perched and the mean sea-level aquifer. The principal source for the public supply of water has for several centuries been the main sea-level water table. The absence of permanent streams or lakes and a considerable runoff into the sea, however, have made water supply a problem, which has been addressed with an intensive reverse-osmosis desalination program. About half of Malta's daily water needs are supplied by desalination plants throughout the islands.

SOILS

Mainly young or immature and thin, Maltese soils generally lack humus, and a high carbonate content gives them alkaline properties. Human settlement and construction developments have altered the distribution and composition of soils. The Fertile Soil (Preservation) Act of 1973 requires that, when soils are removed from construction sites, they be taken to agricultural areas, and level stretches in quarries are often covered with carted soil.

CLIMATE

The climate of Malta is typically Mediterranean, with hot, dry summers, warm and sporadically wet autumns, and short, cool winters with adequate rainfall. More than three-fourths of the total annual rainfall of about 22 inches (550 mm) falls between October and March; June, July, and August are normally quite dry.

The temperature is very stable, with the annual mean in the mid-60s F (about 19 °C) and monthly averages ranging from the mid-50s F (about 12 °C) to the mid-80s F (about 29 °C). Winds can be strong and frequent; the most prevalent are the cool northwesterly (the majjistral), the dry northeasterly (the grigal), and the hot and humid southeasterly (the xlokk, or sirocco). The relative humidity rarely falls below 40 percent.

PLANT AND ANIMAL LIFE

Malta's flora and fauna are typical of the low-lying coastal regions of the Mediterranean. Excessive exploitation of the forests for timber and the clearance of land for construction and agriculture have destroyed much of Malta's woodlands, though a few stands of holm oak remain. Aleppo pine has been successfully reintroduced. Maquis, a scrubby underbrush, is found along valleys and below escarpments and consists of lentisk, carob, olive, bay laurel, and in some places the sandarac gum tree (Malta's national tree). Garigue, a low-growing Mediterranean scrub, is the most common vegetation in Malta and covers much of the country's limestone plateau. The steppe in Malta is dominated by various grasses, thistles, and leguminous and bulbous plants. Reed beds occur wherever there is abundant freshwater, and club mosses, sedges and grasses are found in wetlands. Glassworts, rushes, and seablites are native to the salt marshlands. Sand couch, sea kale, and sea daffodils are found on Malta's few remaining coastal dunes, while golden samphire, rock samphire, and sea lavenders (several of which are endemic) are characteristic of low-lying rocky coasts. Cliffs and coastal screes support many of Malta's native species, which include monotypic genera such as the Maltese cliff-orache (*Cremnophyton lanfrancoi*) and the Maltese rock-centaury (*Palaeocyanus crassifolius*), the latter of which is the national plant.

The native mammals in Malta include a subspecies of the Sicilian shrew and several types of bats. Most of the country's other mammals, including the Algerian hedgehog, Mediterranean chameleon, Etruscan shrew, rabbit, and weasel, have been introduced. Native reptiles include the Maltese wall lizard, the ocellated skink, the Moorish and the Turkish gecko, the western whip snake, and the leopard snake. The only amphibian in Malta is the painted frog, a species endemic to Sicily and Malta. Invertebrates, including insects, arachnids, and snails, are abundant.

Although there are relatively few breeding birds, migrating species are plentiful. Sea birds include the storm petrel and the Mediterranean and Cory's shearwaters. Among the most notable birds are the Spanish sparrow, which is the most common bird in Malta, and the blue rock thrush, Malta's national bird.

ETHNIC GROUPS

Malta's population is composed almost entirely of ethnic Maltese, the descendants of ancient Carthaginians and Phoenicians as well as of Italians and other Mediterranean peoples. Attempts to form a unifying and homogenizing Maltese ethnicity can be traced back to the late 13th century; these efforts were consolidated in the nationalistic discourses of the late 19th and early 20th centuries. Aside from the Maltese population, there are small communities of British nationals, Sindhis, Palestinians, and Greeks on the islands. Since the 1990s influxes of more transient but no less significant groups have arrived from North Africa, the Balkans, and, in

the early 2000s, from countries of sub-Saharan Africa.

LANGUAGE

Maltese and English are the official languages of Malta as well as official languages of the EU. Maltese resulted from the fusion of North African Arabic and a Sicilian dialect of Italian. It is the only Semitic language officially written in Latin script. English is a medium of instruction in schools. Italian was the language of church and government until 1934 and is still understood by a sizable portion of the population.

RELIGION

Roman Catholicism is the official religion of Malta, but there is full freedom of religious belief. More than nine-tenths of Maltese are nominally Roman Catholic; however, only about three-fifths of these practice their faith. The islands are an independent province of the church, with an archdiocese in Malta and a diocese in Gozo. Very small numbers of Maltese are adherents of other Christian denominations or of Islam. There are Roman Catholic cathedrals at Mdina and Valletta, an Anglican cathedral at Valletta, and a mosque at Corradino Heights.

SETTLEMENT PATTERNS

During the 16th and 17th centuries, under the rule of the Knights of Malta

VALLETTA

Valletta, the main seaport and capital of Malta, is located on the northeast coast of the island of Malta. The nucleus of the city is built on the promontory of Mount Sceberras that runs like a tongue into the middle of a bay, which it thus divides into two harbours, Grand Harbour to the east and Marsamxett Harbour to the west. Built after the Great Siege of Malta in 1565, which checked the advance of Ottoman power in southern Europe, it was named for Jean Parisot de la Valette, grand master of the order of Hospitallers (Knights of St. John of Jerusalem), and became Malta's capital in 1570. The Hospitallers were driven out by the French in 1798, and a Maltese revolt against the French garrison led to Valletta's seizure by the British in 1800. After 1814 the city became a strategic British Mediterranean naval and military base of the first order; it was subjected to severe bombing raids in World War II and was the place where the Italian fleet surrendered to the Allies in 1943.

One of the most-notable buildings in Valletta is St. John's Co-Cathedral. Formerly a conventual church belonging to the Hospitaller order, this church is outwardly austere but inwardly sumptuous and is now almost equal in rank to the archbishop's cathedral at Mdina. Built between 1573 and 1578, it was designed by the Maltese architect Gerolamo Cassar. Other buildings by Cassar include the Palace of the Grand Masters (1574; now the residence of the president of the Republic of Malta, the seat of the House of Representatives, and the site of the armoury of the Hospitallers), the Auberge d'Aragon (1571; now home to the Ministry of Finance and Economic Affairs), the Auberge de Provence (1571; now the National Archaeology Museum), and the Castille and León Auberge (1573; now the office of the prime minister). Of the other auberges (lodges built for every langue [nationality] of the Hospitallers), those of France and Auvergne were destroyed in World War II, and that of Italy was heavily damaged. The National Library of Malta was built in the late 18th century, the University of Malta was founded by Pope Clement VIII in 1592, the Manoel Theatre dates from 1731–32, and the National Museum of Fine Arts (opened 1974) is housed in a residence dating from 1571.

Valletta is a city of churches, among them the Church of Our Lady of Victory, which contains the city's foundation stone; St. Paul's Shipwreck Church; and an exquisite octagonal church dedicated to St. Catherine of Italy. Valletta is not an industrial city but is an important commercial and administrative centre. The city's artistic and historical treasures constitute a major tourist attraction. Valletta was designated a UNESCO World Heritage site in 1980.

(Hospitallers), the country evolved as a maritime power, and, by the late 17th century, Valletta and other towns were thriving maritime centres. By the mid-19th century the Maltese lived mainly in the relative seclusion of clustered villages and hamlets; the fragmentation of farm holdings accentuated the individuality of the farming community. The zuntier, a parvis forming part of the church square, was the traditional focus of village life.

During the British occupation of Malta (1800–1964), the growth of the dockyard complex resulted in the ongoing development of new settlements around Grand Harbour. In the 20th century the Sliema region, just north of Marsamextt Harbour, became the most fashionable part of Malta and by the early 21st century had become a commercial and tourist centre. Following the country's independence in 1964, the advent of industrial estates located near major villages somewhat increased urbanization, but higher living standards have given rise to residential developments all over Malta island; its central areas are now densely populated. Overbuilding has been a cause for serious concern, spawning legislation meant to protect the environment.

The essentially rural character of Gozo's many hilltop settlements has been largely preserved in the new housing that has rapidly increased there since the 1990s. Victoria, in the south-central part of the island, is the administrative and commercial centre of Gozo. More rural still is Comino, which is mostly inhabited by tourists.

DEMOGRAPHIC TRENDS

Malta has one of the highest population densities in the world, though the increase in the country's population has somewhat leveled off since the mid-20th century, with a considerable decline in the birth rate. At the same time, the death rate has remained fairly stable, having fallen only slightly, while the infant mortality rate has dropped significantly.

Following World War II, mass emigration was encouraged and even financed by the government because of high unemployment on the islands. From 1945 until the mid-1970s about 150,000 people left Malta and Gozo and settled in other English-speaking countries (the United States, the United Kingdom, Canada, and Australia). By the 1990s, however, emigration had tapered off, and many Maltese expatriates began returning to their homeland.

CHAPTER 14

THE MALTESE ECONOMY

Until the mid-1960s the Maltese economy depended heavily on the British military presence in Malta. In the 1950s Britain began to withdraw its armed forces, which necessitated a drastic diversification of the economy. A series of development plans after 1959 were supported by government grants, loans, and other fiscal incentives to encourage private investment. Import and capital controls, which were extensive until the second half of the 1980s, were progressively dismantled during the 1990s, moving Malta toward a more market-driven economy as the Maltese government pursued a policy of gradual privatization beginning in 1999. Capital controls were fully lifted only when Malta was acceded to the European Union (EU) in 2004. The Maltese economy faces major constraints because of its small domestic market, and it depends on other countries for many imported goods.

AGRICULTURE AND FISHING

Agricultural development is hampered by land fragmentation (that is, plots of land resulting from decollectivization that are too small or too irregularly configured to be farmed efficiently), shallow soils, and lack of adequate water supplies. Most farming is carried out on small terraced strips of land that preclude the introduction of large-scale mechanization. As a result of the growth of urbanization, the agricultural labour force has become increasingly older, and more farming is done on a part-time basis; nevertheless, production has risen gradually because of improved techniques in the cultivation of some crops, especially horticultural ones. The major crops are potatoes, tomatoes, and fruit (especially citrus and drupes). Since the late 1990s there has been a substantial increase in grapevine and olive production. Malta is generally self-sufficient in food production, but beef is mostly imported. Upon the country's accession into the EU, Malta's agricultural sector became competitive.

Fishing is seasonal and, to a large extent, undertaken on an artisanal basis. The common dolphin fish (*Coryphaena hippuras*) and the bluefin tuna (*Thunnus*), however, are caught for export. Aquaculture, introduced in Malta in the late 1980s, has surpassed fishing as a source of income. The European sea bass (*Dicentrarchus labrax*) and the gilthead sea bream (*Sparus aurata*) are grown in floating sea cages, and the bluefin tuna from the sea are fattened on farms for four to six months before export. After Malta joined the EU, Maltese fishermen benefited from funding programs, particularly to promote the export of tuna.

RESOURCES AND POWER

Malta is poorly endowed with natural resources, and its only exploited mineral resource is limestone, which is quarried and used for construction. Offshore oil exploration has been under way since the mid-1990s, but no significant oil reserves have been discovered. Fossils fuels are imported and supply all of Malta's energy. There are thermal power stations on both Malta and Gozo.

MARSAXLOKK

Marsaxlokk (also called Marsa Scirocco) is a village in southeastern Malta. It lies along Marsaxlokk Bay, southeast of Valletta. Marsa means "harbour" in Maltese, and xlokk is a southeasterly wind. The ancient seafaring Phoenicians used the bay as an anchorage for their ships. It was the first landing place of the Turkish fleet in the Great Siege of Malta in 1565. The fortress of Fort San Lucjan—now housing the marine sciences laboratory of the University of Malta—was built there in the early 17th century, and its garrison repulsed a later Turkish landing attempt in 1614. There are remains of extended 18th-century fortifications; the French disembarked their forces at Marsaxlokk in 1798. A fine fishing port, Marsaxlokk also developed as a modern seaside resort. In 1988 Malta Freeport was established to develop the Marsaxlokk port into a regional transshipment centre, linking it with a network of Mediterranean and Black Sea ports. In 1989 U.S. Pres. George Bush and Soviet leader Mikhail Gorbachev chose Marsaxlokk Bay as the venue for talks on the termination of the Cold War.

MANUFACTURING

Industrial development began in earnest in the second half of the 1960s, and by the early 21st century the manufacturing sector was contributing more than one-tenth of gross domestic product (GDP). Since the 1980s the manufacture of computer parts, instruments, and electronics, as well as of a large variety of consumer products (toys, cosmetics, detergents, and foodstuffs), has been important. In the early 2000s, light manufacturing (pharmaceuticals, semiconductors, and automotive and airplane parts, along with software) replaced much of the low-cost labour-intensive production that had earlier played a more important role in Maltese manufacturing. Pharmaceutical production in particular has grown rapidly as a result of the patent law advantages that Malta gained upon EU membership.

Shipbuilding and repair have been the foundation of Malta's economy since the Knights of Malta (Hospitallers) transferred Malta's administrative centre from the medieval inland location of Mdina to present-day Valletta in the Grand Harbour area in 1570. Since the mid-20th century, however, the shipbuilding industry has consistently operated at a loss and had been dependent upon government subsidies. Efforts aimed at engendering financial sustainability during the late 20th century were not successful. Upon EU accession, such subsidies were no longer permissible, and the Maltese government has taken steps to reduce and privatize the industry.

FINANCE

The Central Bank of Malta was founded in 1968. Malta's former currency, the lira, was adopted in 1972. On January 1, 2008, the euro became the country's official currency. The banking system remains highly concentrated, with half of the local commercial banks accounting for about nine-tenths of total loans and deposits. The Malta Financial Services Authority, established in 2002, is an autonomous body and the single regulator for financial services, taking over supervisory functions that were formerly carried out by the Central Bank of Malta, the Malta Stock Exchange, and the Malta Financial Services Centre. The Maltese government encourages and facilitates direct foreign investment, which began to increase in the early 2000s. While the private sector still consists mostly of small enterprises, there are some internationally owned companies operating in Malta, mostly in the pharmaceutical, automotive, and electronics sectors.

TRADE

Malta imports machinery and transport equipment, chemical products, and mineral fuels. The country's main export products are semiconductors, but it also exports other manufactured goods and refined petroleum. Italy, France, the United Kingdom, the United States, Germany, and Singapore are Malta's major trading partners.

SERVICES

Services account for about half of Malta's GDP and employ about three-fifths of the labour force. Tourism is a major source of income and follows a seasonal pattern, with June through October being the peak season. Some notable tourist sites include the ancient megalithic temple Ġgantija on Gozo and the temples of Ħaġar Qim, Mnajdra, and Tarxien on Malta; this group of temples was designated a UNESCO World Heritage site in 1980. Also on Malta are spectacular medieval castles

MDINA AND RABAT

Mdina and Rabat are adjoining towns in west-central Malta, west of Valletta. Possibly Bronze Age in origin, they have Punic, Greek, and Roman ruins. The name Mdina derives from the Arabic word *madīnah* ("town," or "city"). It was also named Notabile in the 15th century, possibly by the Castilian rulers who made it the Maltese capital until the mid-16th century, when Valletta, the new capital, was nearly completed; thereafter it received the appellation of Città Vecchia ("Old City"). Mdina retains intact its remarkable fortifications with a complete set of bastions and contains several 15th-, 16th-, and 17th-century palaces. Its chief building is the Baroque cathedral church of Malta (restored after a devastating earthquake in 1693), said to occupy the site of the house of the Roman governor Publius, whose father was cured by the Apostle Paul. Some damage occurred during World War II, but the city retains its medieval atmosphere.

Rabat is a Semitic word meaning either "fortified town" or "suburb." In Roman times the site of Mdina and Rabat was occupied by Melita, the island's capital. During the Arab occupation of Malta (870 to 1090), the area of Mdina was reduced by moving the southern wall; as a result, portions of Mdina became part of Rabat. There are many Roman ruins, including a partially restored Roman villa that houses a museum of Roman antiquities. Extensive early Christian catacombs, lying beneath the both Mdina and Rabat, contain engraved crosses and agape tables —rock-hewn round surfaces that were used for funerary rituals. There are several cave churches and medieval churches and monasteries. Hospitals are an established tradition in Rabat; Santo Spirito served this purpose for more than 600 years (today it houses the National Archives). The nearby Verdala Palace (1586) was built as a summer residence for the grand masters of the Hospitallers (Knights of St. John of Jerusalem); it was subsequently used by the governors of the islands and, more recently, by the president of Malta.

and cathedrals, as well as the ancient inland capital of Mdina. Tourism has had a major impact on the natural environment of the Maltese islands, and the government has attempted to promote ecotourism.

LABOUR AND TAXATION

The majority of Malta's workforce is employed in the manufacturing and services sectors. Women make up about one-third of the workforce. The public sector is to a very large extent unionized. In the private sector, most large enterprises are unionized. Malta has two chief labour unions—the General Workers' Union, Malta's largest union, and the Union of United Workers—as well as a confederation of smaller sectoral unions, each of which came into being around the mid-20th century. Although unions are independent of political parties, they have tended to occupy a central role in national issues and at times have operated on the

A section of Malta's coastal road along Marsamxett Harbour, in Valletta. Terry Why/Photolibrary/ Getty Images

basis of the party affiliations of their members.

The bulk of government tax revenue comes from a progressive income tax system. There is a value-added tax on consumer goods and services. Taxes on real-estate transactions also contribute to government revenue.

TRANSPORTATION AND TELECOMMUNICATIONS

The island of Malta's road system connects all towns and villages and includes a coast road and a panoramic road. Bus services radiating from Valletta provide inexpensive and frequent internal transportation. Taxis and rented vehicles are available on the island. Most families own automobiles, and the number of cars per household is one of the highest in Europe. There is no railway. Ferry services operate between Malta and Gozo, and Malta and Sicily are connected by both ferry and high-speed catamaran. The national airline, Air Malta, connects Malta with most European capitals as well as with North Africa, the Middle East, and North America. Since 2007 a number of low-cost airlines have offered services to and from Malta.

Malta's telecommunications sector was fully liberalized in 2004, after Malta joined the EU. The mobile phone penetration rate increased substantially in the early 21st century; the majority of the inhabitants now use cellular telephones, while the number of fixed-line phone lines has remained relatively static. Internet usage increased as well. The Malta Communications Authority, established in 2001, is the regulatory body of the telecommunications sector.

CHAPTER 15

MALTESE GOVERNMENT AND SOCIETY

The 1964 constitution, under which Malta became an independent monarchy and parliamentary state, was amended in 1974 to make Malta a republic within the Commonwealth. Malta is currently a unitary multiparty republic. The Maltese parliament consists of a unicameral House of Representatives and is fashioned on the British model. Members of the parliament are elected by proportional representation for five-year terms. An amendment adopted in 1996 guarantees a majority of seats to a party receiving more than 50 percent of the total votes cast in the general election. The parliament appoints the president, who is head of state. The president acts on the advice of the cabinet, which is headed by the prime minister, who is the head of the government.

LOCAL GOVERNMENT

Local government was established in Malta in 1993. The country is divided into 68 localities, 14 of which are in Gozo. Each locality is administered by a local council elected by the residents of the locality by proportional representation every three years. The Department for Local Government oversees the councils.

JUSTICE

Maltese law, which was codified mainly during the period from 1854 to 1873, is largely based on the Napoleonic Code and Napoleonic law. Criminal proceedings and fiscal and

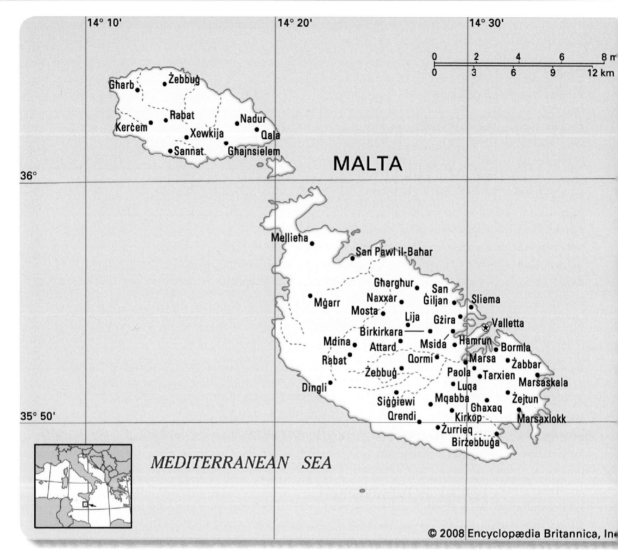

Political map of Malta.

maritime legislation follow English common law, but judicial precedent is not binding. Maltese is the language of the courts. Civil and criminal jurisdiction is almost exclusively vested in the Superior Courts and the Court of Magistrates. The chief justice and other members of the judiciary are appointed by the president on the advice of the prime minister.

POLITICAL PROCESS

Maltese citizens aged 18 and older are eligible to vote. The island is deeply polarized

DOM MINTOFF

Dom Mintoff (born August 6, 1916, Cospicua, Malta—died August 20, 2012, Tarxien, Malta) devoted his political career to Maltese sovereignty, initially pursuing the island's integration within the U.K. and then seeking full independence. He served as a longtime socialist MP (1947–98), the head of Malta's Labour Party (from 1949), leader of the Opposition (1962–71), and prime minister (1955–58; 1971–84). Mintoff received degrees in science (1937) and civil engineering and architecture (1939) at the University of Malta. He was awarded a Rhodes scholarship to Hertford College, Oxford (M.S., 1941; engineering science). Unable to return to Malta during the Italian and German siege of World War II, he worked (1941–43) as a civil engineer in Britain. After he went back to Malta, he practiced as an architect and helped reestablish (1944) the Labour Party, rising to deputy leader and minister of reconstruction (1947–49) before becoming party leader. In response to his platform advocating union with Britain, the British government set up a roundtable conference and agreed to Malta's representation in the British Parliament, but there was serious disagreement regarding economic reforms, and street demonstrations against the British ensued. Mintoff resigned (1958) in protest and then led the Maltese Liberation Movement's drive for independence, which was granted in 1964. After becoming prime minister again in 1971, Mintoff posed financial and other demands to the British and NATO, amended Malta's constitution to transform the country into a republic, expanded the government's involvement in the economy, feuded with the Roman Catholic Church, and drew closer to socialist and nonaligned countries.

in its politics; since independence the two major parties, the Nationalist Party (Partit Nazzjonalista; PN) and the Malta Labour Party (Partit Laburista; MLP), have alternated in power. The Democratic Alternative (Alternattiva Demokratika; AD), also known as the Maltese Green Party, is Malta's third party but has not secured a parliamentary seat since its founding in 1989. Voter turnout in Malta has traditionally been high, with generally more than nine-tenths of eligible voters casting ballots.

SECURITY

Between 1964 and 1972, Malta's main defense dispositions were those contained in a 1964 agreement with the United Kingdom guaranteeing mutual assistance. From 1972 to 1987 Malta followed a policy of nonalignment, and in 1987 a neutrality clause was included in its constitution. Malta maintains its own regular armed forces. Military service is voluntary for those of at least age 18.

HEALTH AND WELFARE

The government of Malta has always played a central role in the provision of health care by offering a comprehensive array of free health services and preventive care to Maltese citizens. State hospitals and clinics are complemented by private hospitals, which have proliferated since the 1990s. Since 1988 the island of Malta has been home to the United Nations International Institute on Ageing (INIA), which has made the island a centre of geriatric care and research.

In 1956 social insurance was introduced to cover employees, the self-employed, and unemployed persons. A comprehensive contributory insurance scheme was introduced in 1972, integrating a variety of earlier legislation. In 1979 this program was enhanced to introduce an earnings-related retirement pension. The 1994 Social Security Act consolidated earlier legislation and also incorporated noncontributory schemes. Until 1986 social security in Malta was administered through three separate laws: the Old Age Pensions Act of 1948, the National Assistance Act of 1956, and the National Insurance Act of 1956. In January 1987 these acts were consolidated into the Social Security Act.

EDUCATION

From the early 1970s until the mid-1980s, the government radically altered the education system, which was previously structured on British models and strongly influenced by the Roman Catholic Church. Compulsory education was extended to include all children ages 5 to 16. The streaming of students by age and intellectual ability and through examinations was at first discarded but later reintroduced. In 2005 Malta's government reformed the education system again and created autonomous regional colleges consisting of primary and secondary schools and junior colleges.

At the tertiary level, a student-worker scheme was introduced in 1978, with students working for six months and studying for six months, thereby linking admission to higher educational institutions to the availability of employment. This system was largely revoked by the Education Act of 1988, and admission to institutions of higher learning is now based completely on competence.

The University of Malta at Msida and the Malta College of Arts, Science, and Technology (MCAST) are the country's principal institutions of higher education. The former was founded as a Jesuit college in 1592, established as a state institution in 1769, and refounded in 1988. It offers courses in most disciplines and has a prestigious medical school. Its modern campus at Tal-Qroqq also houses the International Maritime Law Institute and the Mediterranean Academy of Diplomatic Studies. MCAST, founded in 2000, mainly offers vocational and technical education and has institutes on Malta and Gozo.

CHAPTER 16

MALTESE CULTURAL LIFE

The culture of Malta is reflected in a mixture of Arab and Italian traditions. The Maltese are highly literate and have a deep appreciation of the arts. The Italian painter Caravaggio and the Maltese poet Dun Karm are considered major contributors to art and literature in Malta. Malta's cultural influences stem largely from the country's history of foreign domination and the influence of the Roman Catholic Church. Folk traditions have evolved mainly around the *festa* that celebrates the patron saint of a village, which is marked by processions and fireworks.

DAILY LIFE AND SOCIAL CUSTOMS

As a Roman Catholic country, Malta celebrates Good Friday with colourful processions in several villages. *Mnarja*, the Feast of St. Peter and St. Paul, takes place on the weekend preceding June 29 in Buskett Gardens in Rabat. It is the country's

Colourful floats traverse the streets of Valletta during Malta's annual Carnival celebration. Renault Philippe/hemis.fr/ Getty Images

principal folk festival and is high-lighted by folksinging (*għana*) contests and fried-rabbit picnics. The annual Carnival is celebrated in various villages in Malta, but the main events take place in Valletta, where vigorous dancing displays that include the Parata, a sword dance commemorating the Maltese victory over the Turks in 1565, and Il-Maltija, the Maltese national dance, are performed. Independence Day is celebrated on September 21, and Republic Day is commemorated on December 13.

THE ARTS

In addition to unique Neolithic ruins, Malta contains important examples of its flourishing architectural school of the 17th and 18th centuries, which was essentially Classical with a balanced overlay of Baroque decorations. The Italian artists Caravaggio and Mattia Preti spent several years in Malta, the latter's most important paintings embellishing many of Malta's churches.

In the 20th century many Maltese artists and scholars enriched the country's

DUN KARM

Dun Karm (born Carmelo Psaila, October 18, 1871, Zebbug, Gozo, Malta—died October 13, 1961, Valletta) is considered Malta's national poet and is sometimes referred to as "the bard of Malta," or "the Chaucer of Malta." His work has both romantic and classical affinities. His love of nature and his motherland together with his religious sensibility exemplify the former; his fondness for traditional metre (notably in his sonnets, which are considered particularly fine) exemplifies the latter.

Karm was ordained a priest at the age of 23 and worked as a seminary lecturer and diocesan grammar-school teacher until his dismissal by the ecclesiastical authorities in 1921. He then became assistant director of the National Library, retiring in 1936. He subsequently worked as lexicographer on the official English-Maltese dictionary. Karm was awarded a doctorate of letters by the Royal University of Malta in 1945, and in 1956 he was made a Commander of the Order of the British Empire.

He had already won distinction as a writer in Italian before being invited by the journal *Il-Habib* ("The Friend"), in 1912, to contribute verse in Maltese. Karm influenced several generations of Maltese writers and has been considered instrumental in paving the way for the adoption of Maltese as the official language of the island in 1934. He wrote the lyrics of the national anthem, *Innu Malti* (1923; "Hymn of Malta"). His works have been translated into English, French, Arabic, and Esperanto. Karm himself translated into Maltese the poem *I Sepolcri* (*The Sepulchres*) by the late 18th- and early 19th-century Italian poet Ugo Foscolo, adding a coda of his own.

Karm's home in Valletta, where he lived from 1910 to 1936, became a tourist attraction after World War II.

cultural heritage in the fields of architecture, music, painting, sculpture, literature, and theatre. A vernacular architecture was developed by Richard England and others. The composer Charles Camilleri introduced folk themes into his works, while Maltese literature was enriched by the poetry of the national bard, Dun Karm. An interesting theatrical upsurge led by John Schranz paralleled the emergence of Francis Ebejer as a brilliant playwright. Alfred Chircop and Luciano Micallef have gained prominence with their abstract paintings, Gabriel Caruana has excelled in ceramics, and Anton Agius is a noted sculptor. Maltese soprano Miriam Gauci and tenor Joseph Calleja are internationally renowned.

CULTURAL INSTITUTIONS

Valletta is the centre of many of Malta's cultural institutions, which include the National Museum of Archaeology, the National Museum of Fine Arts, the War Museum, the Manoel Theatre (one of Europe's oldest theatres still in operation), and St. James Cavalier, an old military building that was transformed into an arts centre in 2000. The National Library of Malta dates from the late 18th century and houses a large collection as well as the archives of the Hospitallers. The Maritime Museum and the Museum of Political History are located at Vittoriosa.

SPORTS AND RECREATION

As a consequence of its colonial history, Malta developed a sporting tradition much influenced by its former British rulers, with an emphasis on polo, rugby, athletics (track and field), and especially football (soccer). The national stadium at Ta' Qali is the site of important local and international football matches. A national basketball league was formed in 1960, and there are dozens of amateur teams throughout Malta and Gozo. Swimming, water polo, billiards, and tennis are also popular sports. Malta made its Olympic debut at the 1928 Summer Games in Amsterdam.

MEDIA AND PUBLISHING

Until the early 1990s, Maltese radio and television stations were operated exclusively by a state-appointed body, but a change in legislation opened the way for privately operated broadcasting outlets. Radio and television in Malta are broadcast in several languages. Several daily and weekly newspapers in both Maltese and English are published. Both major political parties operate their own television channel, radio station, and newspaper, while the Roman Catholic Church has its own radio station and newspaper.

CHAPTER 17

MALTA: PAST AND PRESENT

The earliest archaeological remains in Malta date from about 5000 BCE. Neolithic farmers lived in caves such as those at Għar Dalam (near Birżebbuġa) or villages such as Skorba (near Żebbiegħ) and produced pottery similar to that of contemporary eastern Sicily. An elaborate cult of the dead evolved sometime after 4000 BCE. Initially centring on rock-cut collective tombs such as those at Żebbuġ and Xemxija, it culminated in the unique underground burial chamber (hypogeum) at Ħal Saflieni (in Paola, known locally as Raħal Ġdid). Hundreds of thousands of human remains, as well as statues, pots, jewelry, and other artifacts, have been unearthed at Ħal Saflieni, which was designated a UNESCO World Heritage site in 1980.

This culture came to a sudden end about 2000 BCE, when it was replaced by the Tarxien Cemetery culture, a metal-using civilization that practiced a cremation burial rite. This culture in turn was supplanted by the Borġ In-Nadur people (1450–800 BCE), whose settlements were founded on naturally defensible hilltops. Between 900 and 800 BCE, people settled at Baħrija and were known for their distinct type of pottery.

Between the 8th and 6th centuries BCE, contact was made with a Semitic culture. Evidence is scanty, however, and a few inscriptions found on Malta constitute an important indication of a Phoenician presence. For example, a prehistoric temple at Tas-Silġ (near Marsaxlokk) was converted into a Phoenician one. There is more substantial proof of the

Ħal Saflien, an elaborate underground, stone burial chamber on Malta. The rock-hewn tombs were designated a UNESCO World Heritage site in 1980. Werner Forman/Universal Images Group/Getty Images

Carthaginian presence from the 6th century BCE; coins, inscriptions, and several rock tombs of the Punic (i.e., Phoenician) type have been found. It is certain that in 218 BCE Malta came under Roman political control, forming part of the praetorship of Sicily. During the first two centuries of Roman occupation, the islands were allowed to coin their own money, send delegations to Rome, and control domestic affairs. Subsequently they were given the status of Roman municipium. St. Paul,

CULT OF THE DEAD

Among many peoples it has been the custom to preserve the memory of the dead by images of them placed upon their graves or tombs, usually with some accompanying inscription recording their names and often their achievements. This sepulchral iconography began in Egypt, the portrait statue of King Djoser (second king of the 3rd dynasty [C. 2686–c. 2613 BCE]), found in the *serdab* (worship chamber; from the Arabic word for cellar) of the Step Pyramid being the oldest known example. The Egyptian images, however, had a magical purpose: they not only recorded the features of the deceased but also provided a locus for his *ka*, the mysterious entity that constituted an essential element of the personality. The sculptured gravestones of classical Athens deserve special notice, for they are among the noblest products of funerary art. They are expressive of a restrained grief for those who had departed to the virtual extinction of Hades. The deceased are often shown performing some familiar act for the last time. The inscriptions are very brief and usually record only the name and parentage; sometimes the word "farewell" is added.

the Apostle, was shipwrecked on Malta in 60 CE, and, as it is believed, converted the inhabitants to Christianity. Numerous collective underground burial places dating from the 4th to the 8th century CE represent the first archaeological evidence of Christianity in Malta.

CHANGING RULE

With the division of the Roman Empire in 395 CE, Malta was given to the eastern portion ruled from Constantinople (now Istanbul). Until the 15th century, it followed the more immediate fortunes of nearby Sicily, successively under Byzantine rule (535–870 CE) and Arab rule (870–1090); both groups left a strong mark on the language and customs. The Normans and their Swabian successors in the Kingdom of Sicily (1091–1266) had changed Malta's legal and governmental

structures. A short period of Angevin rule (1266–82) was followed by Spanish rule (1282–1530), when the islands were governed by a succession of feudal lords.

HOSPITALLERS

In 1530 the Holy Roman emperor Charles V ceded Malta to the homeless Order of the Knights of Rhodes (subsequently the Sovereign and Military Order of the Knights of Malta), a religious and military order of the Roman Catholic Church that had been without a base for seven years prior. Charles gave them the Maltese archipelago in return for, among other things, the annual presentation of a falcon to his viceroy of Sicily.

The superb leadership of Grand Master Jean Parisot de la Valette prevented Süleyman the Magnificent from

A Knight of Malta (centre, with sword) *relishes the defeat of Turkish forces in the Siege of Malta, in 1565.* Hulton Archive/Getty Images

dislodging the Knights from Malta in 1565 in one of the most famous sieges in history, which ended in a Turkish disaster. What was left of the Turkish navy was permanently crippled in 1571 at the Battle of Lepanto by the combined fleets of several European powers that included the Knights of Malta.

The Knights then proceeded to build a new Maltese capital, Valletta, named after la Valette. The new capital city became a town of splendid palaces and unparalleled fortifications. A hospital of grand dimensions attracted many physically and mentally ill patients from outside Malta. Growing in power and wealth—owing mainly to their maritime adventures against the Ottomans—the Knights left the island an architectural and artistic legacy. Although there was little social contact between them and the Maltese, the Knights managed to imprint

VITTORIOSA

Vittoriosa, in eastern Malta, is situated on a small peninsula just south of Valletta across Grand Harbour. Originally known as Il Borgo, and then Birgu, it was one of the most important towns in medieval Malta. In 1530, when the Hospitallers (Knights of St. John of Jerusalem) arrived in Malta, they resided in and conducted their government from this town. It was strongly fortified and served as the Hospitallers' defense bastion against the Turks in the Great Siege of Malta in 1565. To commemorate the victory over the Turks, the city was renamed Vittoriosa ("Victorious"), although the name Birgu is still used as well. It effectively served as the Hospitallers' capital until replaced by Valletta in 1570. The town continued to develop in the 17th century with commercial facilities and shipyards. Although Vittoriosa was severely damaged in World War II, some of its old fortifications remain, including the historic Fort St. Angelo (870; renovated and extended 1530). The Palace of the Inquisitors and most of the 16th-century *auberges* (lodges of the Hospitallers) also survive.

their cosmopolitan character on Malta and its inhabitants.

MALTA UNDER BRITISH RULE

In 1798 French army officer Napoleon Bonaparte (later Napoleon I) captured the island, but the French presence was short-lived. By the middle of 1800 British troops that had been called in to assist the Maltese had arrived. The French held out for three months before they surrendered the island to the British. The Treaty of Amiens returned the island to the Knights in 1802. The Maltese protested and acknowledged Great Britain's sovereignty, subject to certain conditions incorporated in a Declaration of Rights. The constitutional change was ratified by the Treaties of Paris (1814–15).

Maltese claims for local autonomy were dismissed by Britain, but they never abated. Malta's political status under Britain underwent a series of vicissitudes in which constitutions were successively granted, suspended, and revoked. British exploitation of Malta's military facilities dominated the local economy, and the dockyard became the colony's economic mainstay.

The island flourished during the Crimean War (1853–56) and was favourably affected by the opening of the Suez Canal in 1869. Self-government was granted in 1921 on a dyarchical basis whereby Britain retained control of foreign and military affairs, while a newly created Maltese legislature was responsible for local issues. This agreement was withdrawn in 1933, mostly as a result of Maltese resistance to the imposition of English in lieu of Italian as Malta's official language. As such, Malta reverted to a strictly colonial regime in which full

GEORGE CROSS

King George VI instituted the George Cross, a British civilian and military decoration for "acts of the greatest heroism or of the most conspicuous courage in circumstances of extreme danger." The award, which can be conferred posthumously, is usually given to civilians, although it can be bestowed on military personnel for acts for which military decorations are not usually awarded. The George Cross superseded the Medal of the Order of the British Empire for Gallantry (commonly known as the Empire Gallantry Medal).

The island of Malta received the George Cross in recognition of its inhabitants' gallantry in World War II. Recipients of this award may add "G.C." after their names; the cross ranks second only to the Victoria Cross (the highest British military decoration). The cross is silver, with one side depicting St. George slaying the dragon and with the inscription "For Gallantry"; the other side gives the recipient's name and the date of the award.

The George Medal, instituted at the same time as the George Cross, is analogous to it but is awarded for services not quite so outstanding as those which merit the George Cross. Recipients of this medal can add "G.M." after their names. The medal is silver; one side has the effigy of the reigning British monarch, and the other side has St. George and the dragon with the inscription "The George Medal."

The George Cross medal. Dan Burn-Forti/The Image Bank/Getty Images

power rested in the hands of the governor. During World War II (1939–45) the island underwent intense and prolonged bombing by the Axis Powers but did not surrender. The heroism of the Maltese people was recognized when the island as a whole was awarded the George Cross, Britain's highest civilian decoration.

MALTA SINCE INDEPENDENCE

Self-government was granted in 1947, revoked in 1959, and then restored in 1962. Malta finally achieved independence on September 21, 1964, becoming a member of the Commonwealth and subsequently a member of the Council of Europe. Malta became a republic on December 13, 1974.

The immediate pre- and postindependence period was marked by a hardening polarization between Malta's two major political parties. From 1962 to 1971, Malta was governed by the Nationalist Party (Partit Nazzjonalista; PN), which pursued a policy of firm alignment with the West. In 1971, however, the Malta Labour Party (Partit Laburista; MLP) came to power, embracing a policy of nonalignment and aggressively asserting Malta's sovereignty. The MLP formed a special friendship with China and Libya and negotiated an agreement that led to the total withdrawal of British forces from Malta by 1979. The closure of the British base was celebrated by the Maltese government as the arrival of "real" independence.

The PN returned to power in 1987 and sought full membership in the European Economic Community (later succeeded by the European Union [EU]). But when the MLP took the reins again in 1996, the party froze Malta's application for membership in the EU. The MLP's time in office was short-lived, however, because Prime Minister Alfred Sant called for new elections in 1998 (three years ahead of schedule) after having lost support from his own party. The PN was returned to office in 1998; it reactivated the application for accession to the EU and ushered in major social and economic changes in pursuit of that goal. After considerable political wrangling between the PN and the MLP, Maltese voters in a 2003 referendum chose to join the EU, of which Malta became a member on May 1, 2004. Malta adopted the euro as its currency on January 1, 2008. The PN was again returned to power in 2008, winning the general elections over the MLP by a small margin of votes.In May 2011, Maltese voters approved a referendum recommending the legalization of divorce. Until then, Malta had been the only EU country, and one of only a few countries worldwide, without a divorce law. Legislation permitting divorce was passed by the parliament in June and put into effect in October.

CONCLUSION

Although Cyprus, Greece, and Malta are separated from each other by wide stretches of water (Valletta lies roughly 530 miles [850 km] to the west of Athens, and Nicosia lies roughly 570 miles [920 km] to the east), it is still possible to find similarities throughout the countries' history. Beginning in prehistory and continuing into the modern era, all three have been closely connected to the system of seafaring trade that created a uniquely vigorous exchange of goods and ideas along the shores of the Mediterranean Sea. Possessing natural advantages such as good harbours that made them well-suited to serve as trading centres or military outposts, Cyprus, Greece, and Malta each had extensive contact with its neighbours.

Over the centuries, encounters, both friendly and unfriendly, with Phoenicians, Greeks, Romans, Arabs, and western European Christians left a lasting imprint. The effects of this cross-fertilization are visible, for example, in the exceptionally wide variety of architectural styles on display in each country. The Maltese language, which features Semitic and Romance elements, is another example.

In late antiquity and after, Greece, Malta, and Cyprus seldom enjoyed the freedom to govern themselves independently. For the most part they remained under the direct or indirect control of stronger political and commercial powers. This state of affairs persisted into the modern period, although movements for national self-determination appeared in each country. A Greek rebellion against the Ottoman Empire resulted in the establishment of an independent kingdom of Greece in 1832. Malta and Cyprus, which had come under British control during the 19th century, each negotiated their independence in the 1960s. The countries' fates were, in a way, joined once again by their individual admissions to the European Union; Greece in 1981, and both Malta and Cyprus in 2004.

GLOSSARY

ARCHIPELAGO An expanse of water with many scattered islands.

ECUMENICAL PATRIARCH The male leader of Constantinople given first honor in the Eastern Orthodox Church.

ENCROACH Going beyond limits of propriety to gradually gain the possessions or rights of another.

EXPATRIATE One who has withdrawn from residence in or allegiance to his or her native country.

GOTHS Ancient Germanic people who overran the Roman Empire in the early centuries of the Christian era.

HETERODOX Contrary to or different from an acknowledged standard, a traditional form, or an established religion.

HUNS Nomadic central Asian people who gained control of a large part of central and eastern Europe about 450 A.D.

JUNTA A group of people controlling a government especially after a revolutionary seizure of power.

MOUFLON A type of wild, mountain sheep.

MUNICIPALITY A primarily urban political unit having corporate status and usually powers of self-government.

PARTITION The act of dividing or splitting into parts.

PLEBESCITE A vote by which the people of an entire country or district express an opinion for or against a proposal regarding their government or ruler.

POLYGLOT A mixture or confusion of languages or nomenclatures.

PRAETORSHIP An ancient Roman magistrate ranking below a consul and having chiefly judicial functions.

PROCONSUL A governor or military commander of an ancient Roman province.

RAPPROCHEMENT The establishment of or state of having cordial relations.

REPUBLIC A government having a chief of state who is not a monarch and who in modern times is usually a president.

SCHISM Referring to a formal division in or separation from a church or religious body.

SECULARIST Exhibiting or referencing indifference to or rejection of religion and religious considerations.

SUZERAINTY Referring to the dominion of an overlord or supreme leader.

SYLLABARY A table of written characters, each of which represents a syllable of a spoken language.

SYNOD A church governing or advisory council.

BIBLIOGRAPHY

CYPRUS

GEOGRAPHY

Works that explore some of the pervasive social and economic issues between the Greek and Turkish communities include Vangelis Calotychos, *Cyprus and Its People: Nation, Identity, and Experience in an Unimaginable Community, 1955–1997* (1998); and J.V. Thirgood, *Cyprus: A Chronicle of Its Forests, Land, and People* (1987).

Among the useful discussions of cultural aspects are *J. Paul Getty Museum, Cyprus Before the Bronze Age: Art of the Chalcolithic Period* (1990); and Nancy Sevcenko and Christopher Moss (eds.), *Medieval Cyprus: Studies in Art, Architecture, and History in Memory of Doula Moriki* (1999).

HISTORY

A useful general reference is Farid Mirabargheri, *Historical Dictionary of Cyprus* (2010). For the ancient and medieval periods, works include Arthur Bernard Knapp, *The Archaeology of Cyprus: From Earliest Prehistory Through the Bronze Age* (2013); Nicholas Coureas, *The Latin Church in Cyprus, 1195–1312* (1997); and Peter W. Edbury, *The Kingdom of Cyprus and the Crusades, 1191–1374* (1991, reissued 1994). The modern period and the conflict between Greek and Turkish Cypriots are covered in *Ioannis Stefanidis, Isle of Discord: Nationalism, Imperialism, and the Making of the Cyprus Problem* (1999); Stavros Panteli, *The History of Modern Cyprus* (2005): and Rebecca Bryant and Yiannis Papadakis (eds.), *Cyprus and the Politics of Memory: History, Community, and Conflict* (2012).

GREECE

GEOGRAPHY

Greece's geology is treated in a regional context in Clifford Embleton (ed.), *Geomorphology of Europe* (1984), chapter 16; Derek V. Ager, and in *The Geology of Europe* (1980), chapters 15–16. Individual aspects of the landscape are dealt with in E.G. Mariolopoulos, *An Outline of the Climate of Greece* (1961; originally published in Greek, 1953). J.R. McNeill, *The Mountains of the Mediterranean World: An Environmental History* (1992), includes the Píndos Mountains as one of the case studies.

Classic studies of Greece's people and customs include Ernestine Friedl, *Vasilika: A Village in Modern Greece* (1962); and J.K. Campbell, *Honour, Family, and Patronage: A Study of Institutions and Moral Values in a Greek Mountain Community* (1964, reissued 1974). Timothy Ware (*Kallistos Ware*),

The Orthodox Church, rev. 2nd ed. (1997), is a clear and concise account of the history and theology of the predominant religion in Greece.

The economy is addressed in Persefoni V. Tsaliki, *The Greek Economy: Sources of Growth in the Postwar Era* (1991). Politics is dealt with in Keith R. Legg, *Politics in Modern Greece* (1969); and in Richard Clogg, *Parties and Elections in Greece* (1987).

The remarkable continuities in the Greek language are discussed in Robert Browning, *Medieval and Modern Greek*, 2nd ed. (1983). A comprehensive survey, beginning with the emergence in the 11th century CE of literature in a recognizably modern form of the language, is Linos Politis (Linos Polités), *A History of Modern Greek Literature* (1973).

HISTORY

GREECE DURING THE BYZANTINE PERIOD, C. 300 CE–C. 1453

General surveys of the history of the Byzantine world all include information dealing with Greece at the appropriate junctures. The most useful are George Ostrogorsky (Georgije Ostrogorski), *History of the Byzantine State*, 2nd ed. (1968, reissued 1980; originally published in German, 1940); and J.M. Hussey, D.M. Nicol, and G. Cowan (eds.), *The Byzantine Empire*, 2nd ed., 2 vol. (1966–67), vol. 4 of *The Cambridge Medieval History*; the

latter in particular contains material relevant to the local historical evolution of the various Greek regions.

Works dealing specifically with Greece include Apostolos E. Vacalopoulos, *Origins of the Greek Nation*, trans. from Greek (1970); and Nicolas Cheetham, *Mediaeval Greece* (1981), both of which provide excellent general accounts, the former in particular presenting political, socioeconomic, and ethnic-linguistic issues. A basic reference work that also includes further references is Alexander P. Kazhdan (ed.), *The Oxford Dictionary of Byzantium*, 3 vol. (1991).

GREECE UNDER OTTOMAN RULE, 1453–1831

An overview of the critical four centuries of Ottoman rule is contained in D.A. Zakythinos (Dionysios A. Zakythènos*)*, *The Making of Modern Greece: From Byzantium to Independence*, trans. from Greek (1976). Richard Clogg (ed. and trans.), *The Movement for Greek Independence, 1770–1821* (1976), illustrates the emergence of the Greek national movement through contemporary documents; while *G.P. Henderson, The Revival of Greek Thought, 1620–1830* (1970), focuses on the intellectual revival that preceded the outbreak of the war of independence in 1821.

GREECE SINCE 1831

General histories in English that deal in considerable detail with the 19th and early 20th centuries include Richard Clogg, *A Concise History of Greece* (2002), which, with its authoritative text and illustrations, is a fine introduction. *Journal of Modern Greek Studies* (semiannual), published by the Modern Greek Studies Association, is the premier publication for scholarship on modern Greece; and John A. Petropoulos, *Politics and Statecraft in the Kingdom of Greece, 1833–1843* (1968), is somewhat specialized but important for understanding this formative phase of modern Greece.

Works focusing on Greece in the early 20th century include George B. Leon, *Greece and the Great Powers, 1914–1917* (1974), which focuses on the role of Britain and France in Greece's internal affairs during World War I; George Th. Mavrogordatos, *Stillborn Republic: Social Coalitions and Party Strategies in Greece, 1922–1936* (1983), an indispensable guide to the complex politics of the interwar periods; and John O. Iatrides (ed.), *Greece in the 1940s: A Nation in Crisis* (1981), a collection of scholarly essays on this difficult decade for Greece.

Greek history after World War II is treated in Loring M. Danforth, *The Macedonian Conflict: Ethnic Nationalism in a Transnational World* (1995), an objective account of the "issue," which continues to vex Greeks; Michalis Spourdalakis, *The Rise of the Greek Socialist Party* (1988), which recounts the rise to power of Andreas Papendreou and his PASOK party; C.M. Woodhouse, *The Rise and Fall of the Greek Colonels* (1985), an astute analysis of the military dictatorship of 1967–74, and *Karamanlis: The Restorer of Greek Democracy* (1982), a biography of the politician who twice led Greece toward democracy.

Van Coufoudakis, Harry J. Psomiades, and Andre Gerolymatos (eds.), *Greece and the New Balkans: Challenges and Opportunities* (1999); and Dionyssis G. Dimitrakopoulos *and* Argyis G. Passas *(eds.), Greece in the European Union* (2004), examine Greece in recent times.

MALTA

GEOGRAPHY

Henry Frendo *and* Oliver Friggieri *(eds.), Malta: Culture and Identity* (1994), is a compilation of essays on Maltese language, heritage, art, economy, migration, and more. Malta's physical landscape is detailed in Martyn Pedley, *Limestone Isles in a Crystal Sea: The Geology of the Maltese Islands* (2002).

Maltese folklore is treated in Tarcisio Zarb, *Folklore of an Island: Maltese Threshold Customs* (1998). The role of religion is explored in Jeremy Boissevain, *Saint and Fireworks: Religion and Politics in Rural Malta* (1993).

The Maltese language is analyzed in Joseph Brincat, *Maltese and Other Languages: A Linguistic History of Malta* (2011). Maltese art is featured in Mario Buhagiar, *The Iconography of the Maltese Islands, 1400–1900* (1988).

HISTORY

A general survey of the history of Malta is presented in Brian Blouet, *The Story of Malta*, 3rd rev. ed. (1981). The early period is discussed in J.D. Evans, *The Prehistoric Antiquities of the Maltese Islands* (1971); and David H. Trump *and* Daniel Cilia, *Malta: Prehistory and Temples* (2002).

Anthony Bonanno, Malta: Phoenician, Punic, and Roman (2005), highlights the economic, social, and political achievements of those periods. *Charles Dalli* and *Daniel Cilia, Malta: The Medieval Millennium* (2006), tells the story of Malta from the end of Roman rule to the arrival of the Hospitallers. The period of the Knights of Malta is examined in *Ernle Bradford, The Great Siege: Malta 1565* (1961, reissued 1979). *Joseph Pirotta, Fortress Colony: The Final Act, 1945–1964,* 3 vol. (1987–2001), traces Malta's path to independence.

Ernle Bradford, Siege: Malta to 1940–1943 (1985); and *Charles A. Jellison, Besieged: The World War II Ordeal of Malta, 1940–1942* (1984), focus on Malta's role in World War II. Malta's pursuit of independence is explored in *The Origins of Maltese Statehood: A Case Study of Decolonization in the Mediterranean,* 2nd ed. (2000). *Jon P. Mitchell, Ambivalent Europeans: Ritual, Memory, and the Public Sphere in Malta* (2002), examines Maltese national identity in the years right before Malta joined the European Union.

INDEX